ORCHIDS MADE EASY

The Ultimate Orchid Guide

By Ryan & Laura Levesque

RL & ASSOCIATES, LLC

www.OrchidsMadeEasy.com

Welcome To The Ultimate Orchid Guide

Dear Fellow Orchid Lover,

Welcome! This is Ryan here, and I want to personally welcome you to the Ultimate Orchid Guide. But before we begin, first things first. I've gotta throw out a little disclaimer... growing Orchids can be dangerous to your health. It can be addictive. You can become obsessed :)

In fact, you can probably tell by now that I'm a little obsessed with Orchids myself. So before writing this book, I initiated a massive research project and interviewed over 300 orchid growers (331 to be exact) to find out exactly what information would be most valuable in a book about growing and caring for Orchids.

This book represents literally hundreds of word-of-mouth tips and tricks, which are next to impossible to find in your local bookstore. This the true gold which only comes from years and years of hands-on experience – including all the hard-to-find Orchid information that you can't just find by doing an internet search or heading over to your local public library.

You're in store for a real treat.

How to get the most out of this book:

The book is organized into two main parts. ***Part I*** is organized into topic-specific chapters, with each chapter covering the essentials of a major aspect of growing and caring for Orchids. Part I is structured to provide you with a thorough understanding of all aspects of growing orchids, and is designed so you can go back for quick reference. My recommendation is that you read through Part I from beginning to end at least once, because there are dozens of juicy little tips and secrets tucked away in each chapter, and you never know what nugget of information is going to be the true gold for you.

Part II is organized as a FAQ / Troubleshooting guide, which will be most useful to you whenever you're looking for a quick answer or solution to a specific question or problem. Just jump to the topic you have a question about, and you'll find the answers to your most frequently asked questions conveniently laid out for you right there. In certain cases, you'll be pointed to several parts of the book for more detailed answers.

Also, *if you ordered the special limited* bonus pack, included are several bonuses. As a first bonus, you are also receiving quick reference ***Orchid Cheat Sheets*** for each of the most common varieties of Orchids. Care advice and instructions vary significantly from one Orchid variety to the next, so you'll find these cheat sheets to be an invaluable reference when you're looking for a quick way to just "get the info you need" for your specific Orchid.

As a second bonus, you're also receiving a special ***Orchid Care Calendar*** to help guide you through the seasons, so you know exactly what you should be doing each month of the year to care for your Orchids.

Finally, I've also provided for you within the ***Appendix*** a list of the best resources out there if you'd like to get more information on any particular topic that falls outside the scope of this book. While this book aims to be the most definitive resource on growing and caring for Orchids, there are endless specific issues and advanced topics that we could fill several more volumes. I've personally used and screened every single resource that's included in the book (and I review them on an ongoing basis) to ensure that the information your getting is really top notch.

If you come across any information that you believe is not accurate, feel free to send me an email at Ryan@OrchidsMadeEasy.com. Please note however, that because of the volume of email I receive, while I do read every piece of mail that comes into my inbox, I'm not always able to respond. Finally, if you come across any typographical or grammatical errors in this book, they're here for a purpose. Some people actually enjoy looking for them and we strive to please as many people as possible :)

Okay, I think that's about it. Time to dive right in!

Sincerely yours,

Ryan Levesque

Ryan Levesque

DID YOU KNOW? *The word "orchid" is derived from the Greek word orchis, meaning "testis", and was named so because of their testiculate root or bulb!*

Before we dive right into into the details of growing and caring for your orchids, let's get a few questions out of the way that most people have when they first start growing orchids.

How many orchids are there?

The orchid belongs to the largest family of flowering plants in the world. In fact, there are an estimated 30,000 orchid species recorded and new species are still being discovered on our planet each year. There are also over 100,000 registered hybrid strains with many new hybrids thriving and flowering for the first time. Their range in size, color, shape, and even fragrance make orchids some of the most diverse and beautiful flowering plants on our planet. Despite this variety, identifying an orchid species and/or hybrid is still possible, and I've explained how you should go about doing this later on in the book (*See Chapter 3*).

Not all orchids have a smell. Some have delicate smells of rose, vanilla and jasmine, while others are even known to smell of decay. Check out Appendix I for some of the many wonderfully scented orchids... and the bit about the "World's Stinkiest Orchid."

Where do orchids grow in the wild?

Orchids are found on every continent except Antarctica—some are even native to the Arctic Circle! Roughly 80 percent of orchids are from the tropics of Central America, South America, Asia and Malaysia. (Keep in mind that tropics does not necessarily mean steamy tropical conditions. In fact, many orchids grow in cooler regions where factors like altitude impact their growth cycles.)

So, tell me the truth: Are orchids difficult to grow?

This is by far one of the greatest misconceptions about orchids. If you have someone to walk you through the most important things you need to know, orchids can be a breeze to grow (with the exception of some of the more advanced hybrid varieties). Orchids are extremely sturdy plants and many can be kept in similar indoor conditions alongside your other houseplants.

As I mentioned to you in the *Welcome* section, this book will arm you with everything you need to know about caring for your orchid. If you're just dying to jump ahead, you can skip right over to *Chapters 3-7* to read about the eight most important aspects of orchid care: *temperature, light, humidity, water, fertilizer, pests & diseases, blooming, and potting.*

What are the easiest/best orchids for beginners?

This is a great question! Growing orchids in your home can be extremely rewarding, and sometimes there's just no greater feeling than waking up in the morning and watching your plants thrive, especially when they're in full bloom. But picking an orchid that's easy to work with - especially when you're just starting out - will build your confidence and help take you from "not knowing anything at all" to "hey, this is EASY."

One of the biggest challenges in choosing an orchid, is the fact that there are literally thousands of orchid varieties to choose from... And narrowing down the choices can be a bit daunting. If you're having trouble deciding which orchid you should try growing, I've included a *"Best Orchids for Beginners"* list in the General FAQs in ***Part II*** of this book to help you decide. Of course, the easiest orchid to grow will be the one that's the best match for your particular home/outdoor environment. You'll learn exactly how to assess your environment in *Chapter 3* in this book.

REMEMBER: *Don't forget to check out your* Orchid Cheat Sheets *which have been included for you as a bonus with this book—these concise care sheets detail every aspect of proper orchid care, with specific instructions for each of the most common varieties of Orchids.*

And finally, a little Orchid Trivia (so you can impress your friends):

Did you know that one of your favorite flavors, vanilla, comes from an orchid? It's true! The flavoring comes from the seed capsules of the Vanilla or Vanilla planifolia orchid. (Many flavorings on the market are artificial substitutes.) It was discovered by the ancient Aztecs and introduced to the English in the mid-eighteenth century where it rose in popularity.

World's Tallest Orchid: The Sobralia altissima of Peru can grow up to 44 feet tall. Its flowers measure up to 6 inches across!

World's Smallest Orchid: The Platystele jungermannioides grows primarily in Cost Rica and is only about one quarter of an inch tall. It's tiny flowers grow to only half a millimeter in diameter.

Part I

Ultimate Orchid Care Guide

Chapter 1

Orchid Basics

In this chapter, we'll be covering the following topics:

- Orchid Anatomy 101
- How Orchids Grow
- Where Orchids Grow
- Understanding Orchid Names
- Understanding Orchid Abbreviations
- Common Names For Selected Orchids

Orchid Anatomy 101: The "Body Parts" of Your Orchid

Most orchid flowers are bilaterally symmetrical (or zygomorphic) which is just a fancy way of saying that the right side is often a mirror image of the left side *(See the diagram on the next page)*.

So what makes an orchid different from all other flowers?

The column. The reproductive parts—the stamen (male) and pistil (female)— are fused together to form the single column structure.

How Do Orchids Grow?

There are two basic growth types for orchids—Monopodial and Sympodial.

Monopodial (Latin for "single foot"): Orchids with a main stem that continuously grow upward. Flower spikes, or inflorescences, alternate from one side of the stem to the other. *Angraecums*, *Phalaenopsis*, and *Vandas* are monopodial orchids.

Photo contributed by P. Thongjaj

Monopodial Orchid (*Vanda manudwadee*)

Sympodial (Latin for "many footed"): Orchids that grow sideways along the surface. Psuedobulbs grow from the base (the connecting stem is called a rhizome) and mature at the end of the growing season by flowering. *Cattleyas, Dendrobiums* and *Paphiopedilums* are sympodial orchids.

Photo contributed by A. Pomares

Sympodial Orchid (*Cattleya* hybrid)

Where Do Orchids Grow?

Orchids can also be divided into groups based on where they grow in nature.

The two main groups are Epiphytes and Terrestrials.

Orchid Anatomy 101: The "Body Parts" of Your Orchid

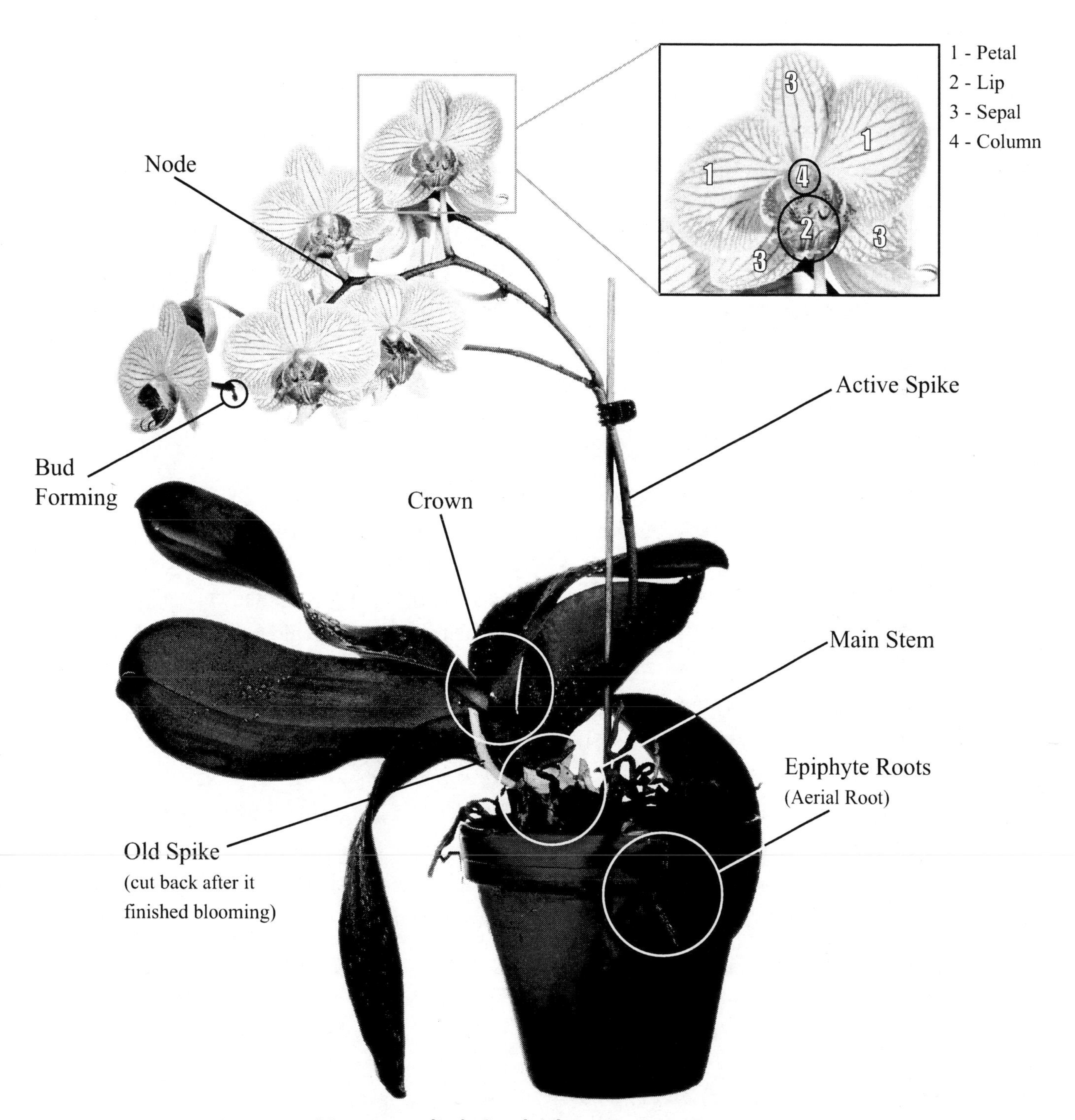

Monopodial Orchid: *Phalaenopsis*

Epiphytes: Air or tree-dwellers. They have thick aerial roots that are covered by a material called velamen (a layer of dead cells). The velamen acts like a sponge and absorbs moisture from the air. These orchids photosynthesize sugars from the sunlight, receive water from rain/dew and absorb nutrients from organic matter that collects around their roots). Most orchids grown by hobbyists are epiphytic. 80% of epiphytic orchids grow in the tropics (tropical & cooler).

Epiphytic orchids are not parasitic or symbiotic—they do not take nutrients from the tree nor does the tree receive any benefit from the orchid. The tree is merely a support and provides good growing conditions for orchids: light, air circulation, proper root drainage, etc.

Terrestrials/Semiterrestrials: Plants that grow on or in the ground. These orchids (like most Paphiopedilums) typically have hairy roots that secure the plant and take food and water from the ground. Unlike Epiphytic orchids, the majority of terrestrial orchids grow in temperate climates. They flower, grow and go dormant depending on the climate. For example, orchids in the Northern Hemisphere typically have a growing period in the late spring and summer and become dormant in the fall and winter (the tubers move underground for protection from the cold).

Other groups:

Lithophytes: Plants that attach themselves to rocks.

Saprophytes: Plants that live off dead or decaying matter. (Very few in number)

Understanding Those Tongue-Twisting Orchid Names:

Orchids can have rather complex botanical names in Latin—but don't worry too much about them. You don't have to understand (or even necessarily pronounce) them to enjoy your orchids. The point of this section is to simply provide you with a brief background that will help you understand the different parts of your orchid's name.

Species Orchid Names

Species orchids are plants created in nature (not hybridized by man).

Each species orchid has two Latin names, a genus name and a species name (In this book, Latin words will always be italicized). In orchids, the genus name is always given first (since this is the larger group) and is always capitalized. Some orchids may also have a third name, the botanical variety. This third name refers to an orchid that varies from the standard species in some way. You'll see the lowercase letters "var." before the lowercase third name.

Think of the genus name like your last name (or family name) and the species name like your first name. Everyone in your family has the same last name, but a different first name. For example, if I were an Orchid my name would be *"Levesque, ryan"* while my father's name would be *"Levesque, paul."* Does that make sense?

Okay, now lets look at real orchid example:
Cymbidium lowianum var. *concolor*

Part of Name	Name	Explanation
Genus	*Cymbidium*	The first name of the orchid (again, like your family name). Always capitalized and italicized. Abbreviated form is Cym.
Species	*lowianum*	The second name. Always lowercase and italicized.
Botanical Variety	*var. concolor*	The third name refers to the botanical variety—if the species is different in some way. Always lowercase and italicized. (This particular variety is the albino form of the species used to create hybrids.)

Hybrid Orchid Names

Hybrid orchids are created by crossing two species—taking pollen from one plant and mating it with another.

Hybrid orchid names can be a lot more complex than species names. The different parts of a hybrid orchid include a Genus, Species, Grex, Cultivar and Award Designation. Like in species orchid names, words in Latin will always be italicized.

Now lets see a real orchid example: *Brassocattleya* Maikai 'Mayumi' HCC/AOS

Part of Name	Name	Explanation
Genus	*Brasso-cattleya*	Combining Brassavola and Cattleya to form Brassocattleya. Always capitalized and italicized. Abbreviated form is Bc.
Species	None	This hybrid has more than one species, so no single one is listed. Hybrids with just one species will have a species name listed, always lowercase and italicized.
Grex	Maikai	All progeny are given a label known as a grex name. This label is always capitalized and not in Latin therefore not italicized.
Cultivar	'Mayumi'	This is a specific selection from the grex. This name is always capitalized, in single quotes and not in Latin therefore not italicized.
Award Designation	HCC/AOS	Highly Commended Certificate from the American Orchid Society.

Award Granting Authorities

The AOS and RHS are the leading award granting organizations. There are many other orchid societies—some specialize in specific kinds of orchids (like the *International Phalaenopsis Alliance*), while others are organized by location. You can do a search on google.com (or ask your local nursery/orchid supplier) to find an orchid society in your local area.

Abbreviation	Society
AOS	American Orchid Society (Based in Florida, USA)
RHS	Royal Horticultural Society (oldest awarding authority, based in London, UK)

Award Designation Abbreviations

The award designation can be divided into two parts: the first part is the abbreviation for the award or certificate and the second part (after the / dash) is the abbreviation for the Society that presented the orchid with the award.

Abbreviation	Award
FCC	First Class Certificate (Extremely high quality, scored over 90 points out of 100)
AM	Award of Merit (Scored between 80-89 points out of 100)
HCC	Highly Commended Certificate (Good, but room for improvement, scored between 75-79 points out of 100)
AD	Award of Distinction (New direction for breeding)
AQ	Award of Quality (High quality new breeding)
CBR	Certificate of Botanical Recognition (Generally awarded first time a species is shown)
CCM	Certificate of Cultural Merit (Awarded to the grower)
CCE	Certificate of Cultural Excellence (Scores more than 90 points out of 100 for Cultural Merit)
CHM	Certificate of Horticultural Merit (Awarded to a plant with exceptional horticultural value)
JC	Judges' Commendation (Exceptional plant that does not fit other award categories)

Example as seen above:
HCC/AOS stands for "Highly Commended Certificate" from the American Orchid Society

Common Orchid Genus Abbreviations

The longer genus names may also be abbreviated. Here is a quick reference list for some of the more common abbreviations you may see being used.

Name	Abbreviation
Brassavola	B.
Brassia	Brs.
Bulbophyllum	Bulb.
Catasetum	Ctsm.
Cattleya	C.
Cycnoches	Cyc.
Cymbidium	Cym.
Dendrobium	Den.
Doritis	Dor.
Encyclia	Ency.
Epidendrum	Epi.
Grammatophyllum	Gram.
Laelia	L.
Lycaste	Lyc.
Miltonia	Milt.
Oncidium	Onc.
Paphiopedilum	Paph.
Phalaenopsis	Phal.
Sophronitis	Soph.
Vanda	V.

Common Names

Some orchids are also referred to by a common name. There are actually only a few orchids that have common names... and when they do, you'll find that the common name most often refers to a group of orchids rather than a specific variety or species. The following is a list of the most frequently seen common names and botanical equivalents:

Common Name	Botanical Equivalent
Bucket Orchid	*Coryanthes*
Lady's Slipper	*Paphiopedilum, Cypripedium, Phragmipedium, Selenipedium*
Moth Orchid	*Phalaenopsis*
Pansy Orchid	*Miltoniopsis hybrids*
Spider Orchid	*Arachnis, Brassia, Epidendrum ciliare, Caladenia*

Chapter 2

Selecting the Perfect Orchid for You

In this chapter, we'll be covering the following topics:

• Where to shop for your Orchid
• Where to obtain a list of recommended Orchid suppliers
• 6 Secrets to Choosing a Healthy Orchid

How do I select an orchid that's right for me?

The easiest (and most important) way to ensure you'll have success with your orchid is to select one that will thrive in your home. I've put together a series of charts in *Chapter 3* to find the best orchid for your particular growing environment. (Keep in mind not all environments are ideal growing conditions, you may need to modify your environment with heaters, artificial lighting or humidifiers to get things just right. You'll learn exactly how you can modify your environment in *Chapters 3*.)

Once you've assessed your home growing environment, you can begin shopping for your ideal orchid.

Where are some good, reputable places to shop for orchids?

Orchids have become so incredibly popular you can find them in local nurseries, discount stores and even on the internet. Generally speaking, you're going to find the best-quality flowers at a specialty Orchid nursery, and one who specializes in a particular species or several varieties. That being said, as a rule of thumb you're also going to pay more for these flowers. You can often find much less expensive alternatives (although limited selection) at your local home and garden retailer, hardware store, or even supermarket. Just be mindful that everything covered in this guide regarding controlling your environment (everything from humidity, to temperature, to light) holds true for the establishment where you purchase your plant.

Orchid Growers/Suppliers

Large selections, experienced and informative growers, but can be a bit pricey.

Local Garden Nurseries

Typically knowledgeable (but not always) with often a more limited selection.

Orchid Shows

Experienced vendors and growers with a wide selection of orchids. See the *Appendix* of this book to learn how to find an orchid show in your area.

Online Suppliers

Check out websites such as **OrchidWeb** http://www.orchidweb.org/marketplace.html and **Orchid Mall** http://www.orchidmall.com.*

Discount Stores/Supermarkets

Inexpensive, often easy to grow/beginner orchids, limited selection, and often maintained in less-than-optimal growing conditions (just think about the icy-cold, air-conditioned produce section of your local grocery store.)

**For an up-to-date list of orchid sellers that I personally use and recommend, please refer to the resources listed in the Appendix of this book.*

IMPORTANT TIP: *Don't forget to get the full name of your orchid and/or hybrid when you make a purchase. You cannot care for an orchid properly without knowing what kind it is. There are a few ways you can try to identify your Orchid if you don't know its name, which I explain later in the book (but none are fool-proof).*

6 Secrets To Choosing a Healthy Orchid

1 ***Leaves:*** Leaves should be stiff and green—do not purchase a plant with brown or black spotted leaves without asking the grower about them if possible.

2 ***Roots:*** Roots should be stiff and light/dusty colored. Black and/or squishy roots are not healthy.

3 ***Pests/Disease:*** Inspect the orchid for fungus and insects before purchasing. Look underneath the leaves and around the pot for any signs of insects or disease.

4 ***Flowers:*** Flowers and buds should be on strong, well-supported spikes. Do not purchase a plant that has fully flowered; purchase a plant with buds yet to open. This will help you understand the flower life of your plant.

5 P***otting Mixture:*** What kind of mixture is the Orchid potted in? If it's an epiphyte (e.g. *Phalaenopsis*) make sure the orchid hasn't been potted in soil. See the section on potting for more information.

6 ***What's in a name, anyway:*** A lot, actually. Orchids require specific care, including everything from potting mixture to fluctuation in daytime and nighttime temperatures. Before purchasing your orchid and taking it home with you, you have to remember that somebody has been taking care of it – rightly or wrongly. One quick and dirty way to get a good idea on whether the orchid you're about to purchase has been properly cared for is to find out the name of the plant you're about to take home. If the plant is simply labeled “orchid” then watch out. When you're asking about the name, you want as specific as possible. The more specific the name, the better chance you're dealing with a supplier who knows what they're doing when it comes to caring for the plant.

IMPORTANT TIP: *You should always quarantine/separate new plants from your existing plants for at least three weeks to make sure the new plants are not carrying any diseases or insect eggs that may hatch.*

Chapter 3

Preparing Your Environment

In this chapter we'll be covering the following topics:

Orchid Identification

• How to identify your Orchid

Temperature

• What Orchids can I grow in my environment?
• The importance of different daytime and nighttime temperatures
• What temperature does my Orchid require?

Light

• How can I tell the level of light in my environment?
• What Orchids are ideal for my lighting conditions?
• What light conditions do my Orchids require?

Humidity

• What humidity levels do my Orchids require?
• How do I raise the humidity levels in my home?

Air Flow

• The importance of proper air flow in your environment

Outdoor Survival

• How to grow your Orchids outdoors

How to get the most out of this chapter:

Orchids, like any other plant, will only thrive when they're in their proper care conditions. Proper orchid care begins with knowing what kind of orchid you have. You actually can use the charts provided in this chapter in two ways:

1. To assess your particular growing environment to find the best orchid for you.
2. To figure out the specific growing conditions you need to provide for your orchid(s).

Identifying Your Orchid:

Already know your Orchid? You can also go right ahead and check out the ***Orchid Cheat Sheets*** that you've received with this book for detailed care requirements that meet your specific orchid's needs.

How do I identify the type of orchid I have?

Have you recently received an orchid as a gift? If so, then you probably want to know how to identify the orchid species you've received.

If your orchid did not arrive with a label, try finding out where the orchid came from. You'll usually be able to get the name with a quick phone call to the nursery or florist or by taking a look at their website.

Most discount stores, local nurseries and florists sell primarily beginner orchids. Refer to the "Best Orchids for Beginners" section in the *General FAQs* in ***Part II*** and/or the ***Orchid Cheat Sheets*** to learn whether you have one of these popular species in your home. The first step is to figure out what genus of Orchid you have, and you should be able to do this by comparing your plant to photographs of plants of the same genus. While you might not be able to identify the exact species, in most cases, knowning the genus will give you enough information to provide proper care conditions for your plant.

If you don't own a beginner orchid or are trying to find the name of the exact hybrid or specialty orchid you have, you can try going a couple different routes.

Try asking an orchid specialist or other orchid growers. You can start with your local orchid society or nursery. Trying posting photos of your orchid on an online Orchid Forums/Boards and ask other members to help you identify your orchid. There are several online and you can do a Google search, but the smartest, most knowledgeable orchid nuts all hang out the following forums:

http://www.orchidforums.net/
http://www.orchidboard.com/community/
http://www.orchidgeeks.com/

In order to post, you'll have to register first, and be sure to introduce yourself if it's your first post. Typically, when you introduce yourself you'll want to include what part of the world you live in, because as knowing (roughly) your environment will make it that much easier for other members to help you out.

One website that has a number of photos organized and labeled by species is http://www.orchidworks.com/ which can be helpful when trying to identify your orchid.

Another resource that I find particularly helpful is this internet orchid species photo encyclopedia, which is a bit more comprehensive. Unfortunately however, the site can be a bit confusing and overwhelming to navigate, but it is still useful: http://www.orchidspecies.com

If you're looking for something better organized and more comprehensive, there are two orchid encyclopedia databases which are like the "rolls-royce" of orchid research tools. These are software programs for purchase, that you install on your computer. They each contain tens of thousands of orchid photos, and information on over 100,000 different orchids, but they don't come cheap. For more information, you can check out the following links:

OrchidWiz Database - ($259.00)
http://www.orchidwiz.com/servlet/StoreFront

WildcattDatabase - ($159.95)
http://www.wildcattdata.com/NewWeb/

Temperature

What orchid(s) can I grow in my climate?

Most orchids enjoy temperature conditions human finds comfortable— which maks them ideal indoor houseplants. However, your orchid will only thrive within its own specific temperature requirements. One of the most unique temperature requirements about orchids is that they require a significant fluctuation between their daytime and nighttime temperatures. In fact, this is one of the biggest reasons why newbie orchid growers sometime can't get their orchid to bloom, or experience a shorter-than-average blooming periods.

Heaters and coolers can be used to regulate these temperatures if necessary—just be sure to follow the other orchid care requirements for your orchid relating to light and humidity levels.

Orchids are usually classified into three different temperature categories. The temperatures below reflect ideal nighttime temperatures. Daytime temperatures should be at least 15ºF (9.5ºC) higher.

The three temperature categories for Orchids are:

Cool:
45ºF to 55ºF (7.2ºC to 12.8ºC)

Intermediate:
55ºF to 60ºF (12.8ºC to 15.6ºC)

Warm:
65ºF (18.3ºC) or higher

To evaluate the growing conditions of your home, use a maximum/minimum thermometer to get an accurate reading of the high and low temperatures (day/night) in your growing area (which may include indoor—windowsill, bathroom, outdoor temperatures). Don't forget to consider the temperature changes across different seasons, and be mindful that if you're placing your flower on a windowsill, the temperature may be significantly different from the rest of the room or house.

To find the required temperature range for your particular orchid, please refer to the chart below:

Temperature Chart

This chart features ideal temperatures (nighttime minimum). The ideal daytime temperature is about 15ºF (9.5ºC) higher than the nighttime temperature.

Cool (45ºF-55ºF/7.2ºC-12.8ºC)

Cymbidium
Dendrobium
Odontoglossum

Cool (45ºF-55ºF/7.2ºC-12.8ºC) to Intermediate (55ºF-60ºF/12.8ºC-15.6ºC)

Cymbidium
Dendrobium
Encyclia
Masdevallia
Miltoniopsis
Zygopetalum

Intermediate (55ºF-60ºF/12.8ºC-15.6ºC)

Aerangis
Cattleya and hybrids
Cymbidium
Dendrobium
Encyclia
Epidendrum
Laelia
Maxillaria
Miltonia
Oncidium
Paphiopedilum
Phragmipedium
Vanda
Zygopetalum

Intermediate (55ºF-60ºF/12.8ºC-15.6ºC) to Warm (65ºF/18.3ºC or higher)

Aerangis
Amesiella

Angraecum
Ascofinetia
Brassavola
Cattleya
Dendrobium
Epidendrum
Neofinetia
Neostylis
Oncidium
Rhynchostylis
Vanda
Vascostylis

Warm (65ºF/18.3ºC or higher)

Angraecum
Phalaenopsis
Vanda

What happens if the temperature is too cool or too warm?

Too Cool:

Orchids in cooler than recommended conditions may be more susceptible to disease, have slower growth, and may suffer from "bud blast"—when buds fall off the stem before they have a chance to open.

Too Warm:

Orchids can survive short periods of extreme heat if the humidity is high enough. Prolonged periods of extreme heat will result in the slowing, even stopping of growth, wilting flowers and buds and shriveled leaves and stems.

If you find your flower experiencing any of these symptoms, when diagnosing the cause of your orchid's problems be sure to first confirm that your orchid is being kept within its optimal temperature range. Adjusting the temperature of your environment is a simple fix, and you can often do it without having to crank up the heat or air conditioning too much simply by finding a naturally warmer or cooler location within your home. You can figure out the best location in your home temperature-wise by moving around a min/max thermometer to compare different areas. Just be sure to take into account daily & seasonal temperature fluctuations if you test different locations over time. If you don't have a min/max thermometer you can pick one up for under $20 at your local hardware store. Just do a Google search for "min max thermometers" because there are a whole range of options.

Light

How much light does my orchid need?

Another important factor in orchid care is light intensity. Most orchids are happy in indirect light. You do not want to place your orchid directly under the hot sun—the temperature and humidity levels (especially in the summer) can potentially kill your plant. If your orchids are on a windowsill, a bright window can simply be shaded with a sheer curtain.

It's important to understand that when we're talking about light, what we humans consider to be "bright" and what is considered bright with respect to orchid care are two very different things. This section will help you determine the optimal light conditions in your home for your orchids.

How can I measure the light in my home?

Traditionally, (and if you've read any other books on Orchids) light is measured in units of measurement called "foot-candles" abbreviated *fc*. I won't get into the details of how the measurement is derived here, but there are some fairly expensive scientific instruments used to measure light intensity with great accuracy. But for our purposes, an expensive instrument really isn't necessary. In fact, there are two simple ways for you that you can determine the light intensity of your environment.

But before we get into that, you should first know that orchids can be divided into three different light intensity categories: Low, Medium and High Light. When translated into *fc* , this equates to the following:

Low:
1,000 to 1,500 fc

Medium:
1,500 to 3,000 fc

High:
3,000 to 4,500 fc

**Please keep in mind that these levels are for mature plants and the high end of the light table is for a limited time during the brightest time of the day (typically around noon).*

The "Quick and Dirty" Light Test:

You can actually get a pretty good assessment of the light levels in your home simply by shading your plant with your hand and evaluating the intensity of shadow cast on your plant.

Low light shadow test:
No shadow will be visible when you hold your hand 1 foot above the orchid's leaves or surface where the orchid will sit.

Medium light shadow test:
A light grey shadow will be visible when you hold your hand 1 foot above the orchid's leaves or surface where the orchid will sit.

Bright light shadow test:
A dark shadow will be visible when you hold your hand 1 foot above the orchid's leaves or surface where the orchid will sit.

The Slightly More Complicated "Camera" Test:

This test is slightly more complicated, but for you purists out there looking to get a more accurate, detailed reading you can fairly easily measure light using a manual SLR camera. Here's what you need to do:

1. Set your camera at 25 ASA
2. Set your shutter speed at 1/60 of a second
3. Place a white sheet of paper where the leaves of your plant would be
4. Focus on the white sheet of paper from a distance of 1 foot
5. Make a note of the f/stop shown in the viewfinder
6. Use the following chart to estimate the approximate light intensity

f/2 = 100 fc
f/2.8 = 200 fc
f/4 = 375 fc
f/5.6 = 750 fc
f/8 = 1,500 fc
f/11 = 2,800 fc
f/16 = 5,000 fc.

Just to give you an idea of sample light intensity, I used the camera method to measure light intensity in my home, in our south-facing kitchen (a very bright room) and our living room, which has both east and north-facing windows. I took the measurements on a bright day in late August, at noon. Here were my readings:

	South Window	East Window	North Window
Against the unscreened windowpane	6000	800	400
Against the screened windowpane	4000	500	250
1 foot away from the window	3000	400	*Not measureable*

So you can see that on a given day, at the same time of day that light intensity will vary dramatically from one side of your home to the other. Obviously, these are just reference points and you'll want to do the same assessment of your own environment.

What level of light does my Orchid require?

In order to get your Orchid to grow and bloom, you need to ensure that you're providing it with at least its minimum light requirement. In a typical home, here's where you should think about placing your plants:

Most low light orchids:

- Placed on an East-facing windowsill
- Within 1 foot of a West windowsill
- Within 2 feet of a South windowsill,
- Within 1 foot of a South windowsill if shaded by plants, and/or under artificial lights.

Most medium light orchids:

- Placed on a West-facing windowsill
- Within 1 foot of a South windowsill

Most high light Orchids:

- Placed on a South-facing windowsill, or within 1 foot of a South windowsill (as long as they do NOT get direct sun in the middle of the day.)
- High light orchids will thrive in bright greenhouses, under artificial lights and on very bright south-facing windowsills.

Light Chart

The following chart identifies the light requirements for selected orchid varieties.

Low Light:

(e.g. Two 40-watt florescent lamps or an east-facing windowsill are ideal)

Paphiopedilum (not including strap-leaf multiflorals)
Phalaenopsis
All seedlings

Medium Light:

(e.g. Shaded greenhouse, east-facing window or four-tube 40-watt) florescent light.

Amesiella
Ascocenda
Ascocentrum
Ascofinetia
Brassavola
Brassia
Cattleya (and hybrids)
Cymbidium (some varieties)
Dendrobium (some varieties)
Epidendrum
Laelia
Leptotes
Masdevallia
Miltonia
Miltoniopsis
Neofinetia
Neostylis
Odontoglossum
Oncidium
Paphiopedilum
Phragmipedium
Rhynchostylis
Zygopetalum

***REMEMBER:** Don't forget to consider the size and/or type of window you have. For example, bay windows provide plants with more sun than regular windows while windows below an overhanging roof may experience more shade than a window without an overhanging.*

Bright Light:

(e.g. Bright greenhouse, very bright south-facing window, metal halide lamps or VHO (very-high-output) fluorescent lamps.)

Angraecum
Cymbidium (some varieties)
Dendrobium (some varieties)
Vanda

Where should I position my orchid relative to the sun?

Ideal Window Directions

South-Facing:

The brightest window conditions. These windows are ideal for orchids that need bright light. Medium light orchids can be placed on south-facing windows if they are placed further from the window or if the window is diffused with a curtain. Do not place the orchid in direct sunlight and keep a constant watch on the temperature as this location may get too hot during the summer. A south-facing window is ideal during the winter when days are shorter and darker.

***IMPORTANT:** Flower spikes always grow in the direction of the best light. It is very important that you do not move the plant's orientation once the flower spike reaches 12 inches. The spike will try to reorient itself to the best light again and this will result in a twisted and distorted spike. You can reorient your orchid's position once the flowers have opened.*

East-Facing:

This direction offers bright, but not too hot, morning sunlight. Most orchids (except bright light orchids) will thrive in east-facing windows for most of the year (move them to a south-facing window if possible during the winter months).

What will happen to my orchid if it isn't receiving the right amount of light?

Your Orchids will adapt to their environment, to some degree. So if you have a medium light orchid, and you're maintaining it on the high end of low light conditions, you may be able to get it to grow and bloom. However, if you have a bright light orchid, you're going to have a real hard time getting it to bloom if you're keeping it on an East-facing windowsill, for example.

Orchids will tolerate light conditions on the high-end of their recommended level, provided that you increase the frequency of watering, add slightly more fertilizer, and if possible increase the air flow to help keep the plant cool. But increasing water frequency, don't go to the extreme. For an orchid that requires watering once a week you might water it once every five days – not once every other day.

Any damage due to too little or too much light will be seen in your plant's leaves.

Too Little Light:

Leaves will darken and become soft. The orchid may also suffer from stretching—a condition that affects some orchids such as phalaenopsis or vandas in which the distance between younger leaves is longer than the distance between the older leaves. New orchid leaves should be the same shape and size (they can also be larger) than the older leaves. Some orchid leaves may grow thinner as a result of too little light.

Too Much Light:

Orchids exposed to too much light will have yellow-green leaves. Intense light exposure may also overheat the leaves and result in sunburn. Sunburn spots are brown and round or oval in shape. A few sunburn spots on the leaves will not do any major damage, but plants can be killed if the damage covers a large area or if the center of the plant is sunburned.

Finally, what do I need to be most careful about when it comes to light?

To sum things up: The risk of improper light is that you'll have stressed plant on your hands. Basically, when a plant is stressed it can fail to grow, and often will fail to flower. So to avoid exposing your orchid to unnecessary stress due to improper light, you'll want to make sure you're taking the following precautions:

1. Avoid direct sunlight. Very few orchids will tolerate direct sunlight except maybe early in the morning or near sunset.

2. When growing in South / South-East light: Particularly if you're growing in a greenhouse, keep in mind that your orchids will require some shade, at least during the brightest part of the day.

3. Remember there is a significant reduction in light from autumn to winter, and you'll want to accommodate for this during the less bright winter months. You can supplement the lack of adequate natural light from October to February with artificial lights.

4. Finally, help your plants out by making the transition from one season to another as gradual as possible. Sudden changes in the environment will lead to unnecessary stress – just think about what it feels like to wake up in a dark room and suddenly open the shades to full bright sunlight! Make sure to ease your orchid into any change in your lighting conditions.

Humidity

How much humidity does my orchid need to survive?

Orchids LOVE humidity. Most orchids thrive in high humidity conditions—think 50% relative humidity or higher. In fact most Orchids prefer humidity levels between 60-80%. These humidity levels are necessary for your plants to perform at their best and reward you with blooms that stay perfect for the longest period of time. Unfortunately, most homes, especially those in cold conditions or with blowing air conditioning or heat units, have a relative humidity between <10-20%.

How do I raise the humidity for my indoor plants without peeling the wallpaper off the walls?

Temperature, light intensity and high humidity can all be achieved in greenhouses, but don't worry, you don't need one to have beautiful orchids. You have several options for raising humidity levels indoors.

1. Orchids can be kept in naturally damp areas of the home like basements and bathrooms as long as temperature and lighting conditions are met.

2. For orchids placed in other parts of the home (like windowsills) you can:

• Use a humidifier, evaporative-pad humidifiers and/or mist humidifiers will work. (Many experienced growers prefer evaporative-pad humidifiers over mist humidifiers because mist humidifiers can leave mineral deposits on your plants.)

• Mist your plants (do not soak) several times a day. Like mist humidifiers, the water may leave mineral deposits on your plants. You can wipe your leaves gently if you notice any deposits. See Chapter 4 to learn a few home remedies that will remove these deposits. You'll also want to be careful not to over-mist your plants, because this can promote bacteria and fungus.

• Grow your plants on a humidity tray—fill tray with water and place your orchid on the grate above the tray. The humidity tray will elevate your plants above the water and it is easy to clean. You can also make your own humidity tray using pebbles. Fill a shallow tray with water and pebbles and then place your pot on the pebbles. You do not want the potting material and/or pot to soak in the water. Do keep the tray/pebbles clean to ensure mold and/or insects do not harm your plants. Ideally, you'll want to keep half a dozen plants or more grouped together, because the humidity from a tray with a single plant will disperse very quickly. Grouping the plants together will create a "micro climate" trapping the higher levels of humidity.

Air Movement

Do I really need to run a fan next to my orchids?

Orchids in nature benefit from gentle winds, so it is no surprise that plants in your care will also need adequate air flow. Adequate air flow ensures that the temperature, moisture, even carbon dioxide levels around the plant distribute evenly. A breeze from an open window, ceiling fan or oscillating fan will provide enough air movement for your orchids to be happy. The air flow should be strong enough to sway your leaves just slightly.

Outdoor Survival

Is ok to grow my orchids outdoors for part of the year?

You may find that your orchid may thrive in your natural outdoor environment, for example, some orchids can live outdoors in Florida, Texas and California for most if not the entire year. If you live in an area that experiences freezing temperatures in winter, you may have no option but move your plants indoors until the harsh weather passes. Fortunately, you can enjoy your plants outdoors in the summer when the temperature rises and the humidity levels increase. The summer sun, however, can be particularly harsh, but you can protect your orchid from the sun's rays by placing them in a naturally shady location.

Shadehouses are also great environments for year-round or summer growing. These can be built in any size (depending on how large you want it/how many orchids you have) from wood lath or shading fabrics (shade levels of 50-60% are ideal for summer).

Balancing your orchid's temperature, lighting, humidity and air movement needs is key to their survival. The following tips will help you achieve a better balance.

• Balance overly bright light/hot temperatures with higher humidity. (Mist more often).

• Balance cool temperatures with less water.

• Balance high humidity levels with more air circulation. (Prevent disease/insects/moisture problems) .

Chapter 4

Watering & Fertilizer

In this chapter, we'll be covering the following topics:

Watering

• How much water you should give your Orchid
• How often to water your Orchid
• What time of day to water your Orchid
• What kind of water is okay to use
• The proper technique for watering your Orchid
• How to know if you've over or under watered and what to do about it

Fertilizer

• What kind of fertilizer your Orchid requires
• Different fertilizer options
• How to know if you've over-fertilized and what to do about it
• The "Secret" 100% all-natural, all-in-one Orchid Fountain of Youth" and Growth "Steroid"

Watering Basics

How much water should I give my orchid?

"How much water does my orchid need?" is one of the most frequently asked questions from new, even experienced, orchid owners. Unfortunately, there is no easy answer to this question. Many external factors must be taken into account to determine the right amount of water your specific orchid needs. This chapter will show you exactly what you need to know to water your plant properly.

IMPORTANT: Overwatering is one of the leading causes of damaged and killed orchids.

You can assess just how much water your orchid needs by taking notice of these factors:

Type of orchid:

Different orchids have different water requirements; therefore, the only way to know how much water your specific orchid needs is to determine what kind of orchid you have.

In general, *Miltonias, Phalaeonopsis* and *Paphiopedilums* orchids enjoy continuously damp conditions while *Cattleyas* and *Dendrobiums* need to dry out between waterings.

Pot: Clay or plastic?

The type of pot your orchid is growing in plays a large part in your plant's watering schedule. Water evaporates from clay pots much faster than it does from plastic pots. This means that plants in clay pots will be watered more often than those in plastic pots.

Simply put, plastic pots are good for orchids that prefer damp conditions while those that need to dry out between waterings will do better in clay pots.

Potting Matter:

Like pots, the potting matter you use for your orchids will retain water differently. For example, moss stays wetter much longer than bark does. An orchid with moss potting matter would require water less often than an orchid potted in bark. You can read more about potting materials in *Chapter 7*.

Environment:

Your orchid and potting matter may dry out faster if the temperature is too hot, the light is too bright and/or if the humidity is too low: add water more often if you find it is evaporating quickly. Don't forget to keep these factors in mind to make sure your plant is receiving adequate water.

Watering Quick Rules of Thumb:

- *The potting material should never be "soggy"*
- *But water potted plants sufficiently to prevent them from becoming bone dry*
- *Small pots (5" or less) need more watering than big pots (6" or more).*
- *Clay pots will evaporate more and dry out more quickly than plastic pots of the same size.*
- *Refer to your Orchid Cheat Sheets for orchid-specific watering instructions.*

How often should I water my orchid?

This is going to vary based on the factors explained in the previous section of this chapter. You should follow the quick rules of thumb, but you can simplify your watering schedule by placing the same orchids in the same types of pots and potting matter so that you can water them all on the same schedule. For example, you'll know that your Phalaenopsis in plastic pots will need watering every X day(s) while your cattleyas in clay pots may need watering every Y day(s).

What time of day should I water my orchid?

Water orchids early in the day or afternoon. Orchids need time to dry before the temperatures cool at night as they are more susceptible to disease if they remain wet in cooler temperatures. Also, you should try to only water on sunny days if possible. If the weather is cool, wet, and rainy, you'll be better off waiting an extra day or two before watering.

What kind of water is okay to use?

In their natural environment, keep in mind that orchids are watered naturally with rain water, and when watering your orchids, the quality of your water is extremely important. Tap water is usually okay, but you have to be aware of a few factors:

1. If your water is hard, which means that the mineral content is high, or for our purposes above 120 PPM – then the water will leave hard deposits on the leaves of plants. This may clog the pores of the leaves and prevent respiration / perspiration. Well water is typically hard. If you're using hard water, you should periodically wipe the leaves of your plants with distilled water, or use one of the techniques that I describe later in this chapter.

2. Be careful with water that has been softened. There are basically two products used for softening water: salt and potassium chloride. Salt adds sodium to the water and this can be lethal to your plants. Potassium chloride however won't cause harm to your Orchids.

If you want to provide the best care possible for your orchids (although it can be a bit of a hassle) rain water is usually the safest and best option, unless you're in an area known to produce acid rain. Normally, rain water is typically slightly acidic – with a PH factor of 6.4 to 6.8. You can collect rain water with several receptacles placed outdoors, and store the water in emptied plastic milk gallon containers. To make things easier, awhile back we created a "sprinkling can" cap by poking a few holes in one of the plastic milk covers, and just use the gallon containers directly to water our plants.

If rain water isn't possible to gather, you can also use the water gathered in a dehumidifier. For example in more humid climates, dehumidifiers are often used in areas prone to mold such as basements and garages. Just remember that you don't want to be using a dehumidifier where your orchids are being kept, because they basically need as humid an environment you can provide for them.

How do I actually water my orchid? Are there any special techniques I should know about?

Always use room temperature or lukewarm water. Hot or cold water can cause injury to your plant. Also, you should use some type of water diffuser (to soften the flow if you are using a hose) or a sprinkling can. You will need to water your orchid thoroughly so that water and excess fertilizer pours out from the bottom of the pot. Do make sure your pot can continue to drain excess water if needed. NEVER let your orchid pot sit in water. This can lead to root rot and unwanted bacteria and fungus—all problems that can kill your plants.

I typically bring my plants to the kitchen and water them over the sink to ensure that they have a good thorough rinsing, and make sure that all excess water has a chance to drain through. When I'm through, I make sure there is no water that has settled on or between the leaves, as this can lead to rot or disease. There are a couple easy ways to get rid of any excess water:

The "wipe" method

Pretty straightforward – just take a dry cloth and wipe over the leaves.

The "blow dry" method

For smaller, tougher to reach areas. simply take a drinking straw and use your mouth to blow focused air on the wet areas.

The "Q-tip" method

For toughest to reach areas, take a cotton swab or "Q-tip" and dab all those little nooks and crannies.

How do I know when my orchid needs water?

One of the fastest ways to judge whether your plant needs more water or not is to get a rough understanding of how heavy your plant is when it is saturated with water. You can pick up your orchid again in a day or two and see just how heavy it remains. Your plant will get lighter as more of the water either absorbs or evaporates. Keep a mental note of your orchid's weight so that next time you'll know simply by picking it up that it needs more water.

You can also determine whether your plant is damp or dry by sticking your finger or a bamboo skewer into 1-2 inches of the potting matter. If you have a Phalaeonopsis (or other orchid that needs damp potting matter) and find that the potting matter is dry, you'll know that it is time to water. The bamboo skewer will come out cool or moist if the potting matter is still damp.

Over or Under: How do I know if I'm overwatering or underwatering?

Both overwatering and underwatering can cause damage, even lead to killing your orchid.

Your orchids will definitely show signs of water damage. For instance, pleated, pluckered, soft, yellow and droopy leaves are all signs of underwatering. Other orchids may suffer from shriveling pseudobulbs and bud blast (when the buds fall off). Unfortunately, these symptoms can also appear if the orchids are overwatered or exposed to hot temperatures for long periods.

Therefore, the best way to determine whether your orchid is sick due to overwatering or underwatering is to remove the plant from the pot and look directly at the roots. This is a must if you want to keep your orchid healthy.

How do I remove my orchid from its pot to examine the roots, without damaging the plant?

Removing your plant temporarily from its pot will not do any damage—keep in mind that this is the best way to evaluate the health of your orchid's roots. In order to check the health of your plant's roots, you should follow this step-by-step process:

Step 1:

Turn the orchid/pot, upside-down with one hand held over the potting material.

Step 2:

Tap the bottom of the pot and/or use a knife or other thin object to lightly scrape around the edges of the potting matter. Gently remove the orchid from the pot.

Step 3:

Take a good look at the roots to determine your orchid's health:

Signs of Overwatering

Soggy, dark, mushy, rotting, or foul smelling roots are a clear sign of overwatering.

Signs of Underwatering

Dry and shriveled roots will be seen if your plant has not gotten enough water. Look at the potting matter to determine if this is the cause of the problem—coarse potting materials may interact poorly with roots and lead to dehydration. If the potting matter is fine, you simply need to increase your watering frequency.

Problem: My orchid has been overwatered, now what?

First you need to determine the extent of the damage. If your roots are only slightly damaged, you can simply repot your orchid in fresh potting matter (see Chapter 7 for details) and adjust your watering schedule so that you water your orchid less often.

If the damage is severe and you see that most of your orchid's roots are soggy, you'll need to do a bit of orchid surgery to bring your plant back to life. Use a sterilized single-edged razor (sterilize your tools before use so that you don't spread disease) to cut off all of the damaged roots. Trim off any sign of damage, treat the roots with a fungicide and then repot your orchid—follow the steps outlined in *Chapter 7*. The roots will need time to develop new growth, so water your orchid very lightly (less than normal)—you can mist your orchid daily to keep your leaves happy. Learn more about how to remove/treat diseased roots on in Chapter 5.

Problem: My orchid has been underwatered, now what?

The procedure for helping an underwatered orchid is similar to dealing with an overwatered orchid. Determine the severity of the problem. An orchid with only slightly damaged roots can be repotted in fresh matter as is. This will give you an opportunity to choose a different potting matter if needed.

One that has major root damage will need to be trimmed in order to be saved. Use a sterilized single-edged razor (sterilize your tools before use so that you don't spread disease) to cut off all of the damaged roots. Trim off any sign of damage and then repot your orchid following the steps outlined in *Chapter 7*. You can repot your orchid in new potting matter if you need to and/or adjust your watering schedule so that your orchid gets the necessary amount of water.

Can I do something to protect cut roots?

Yes, cinnamon and Listerine (original gold colored) can be applied to the recently cut portions of your roots as home remedies to protect broken or cut roots. See *Chapter 5* to learn more.

How can I remove hard water spots on my orchid's leaves?

Forget about using harsh commercial products. Pineapple juice and milk can be used to rise off residue—use it straight and do a second rinse or wipe with a damp rag. Another wonderful home remedy is mayonnaise—dilute it with water and wipe it over the leaves to remove deposits and add shine to your leaves. Wipe away any excess with a damp rag if necessary.

Fertilizer

One important thing to remember when talking about fertilizer, is that fertilizer is not food. Fertilizers act as energy boosters to help make the photosynthesis (food processing) of your orchid more efficient.

What kind of fertilizer does my orchid need?

Orchids require specialized orchid fertilizer—not regular houseplant fertilizer, not rose fertilizer, but fertilizer specifically made for orchids.

All fertilizers contain Nitrogen, Phosphorus, and Potassium as their principle ingredients. These are commonly referred to as N-P-K, and expressed in numbers with their % content within a given fertilizer. So a 30-10-10 fertilizer is 30% Nitrogen, 10% Phosphorus, and 10% Potassium.

Think of this section as your orchid fertilizer checklist, you'll want to look for the following in your orchid fertilizer label:

Orchid Fertilizer Checklist

- *Nitrogen (total amounts of 20% or less are sufficient)*
- *Nitrate nitrogen or ammoniacal nitrogen (NOT urea, because nitrogen derived from urea is not readily available to Orchid plants)*
- *Phosphorus (any amount)*
- *Supplementary calcium (up to 15%)*
- *Magnesium (up to 8%)*
- *Trace elements like sodium, iron, copper, etc.*

The Role of Nitrogen:

Nitrogen is necessary for the plant to grow, but if you use excess nitrogen in your fertilizer your plants will grow excessively in size, and can often delay flowering.

The Role of Phosphorus:

Phosphorus is believed to regulate many activities, including encouraging root growth and inducing and stimulating flowering. A phosphorus can lead to stunted growth and dark green leaves on your plants.

The Role of Potassium:

Potassium is necessary for healthy growth, and a potassium deficiency can result in dwarfness.

When it comes to fertilizers, most orchid growers will recommend using inorganic fertilizers (although there is one BIG exception, one of the true "secrets" to growing exceptionally stunning orchids, which I divulge later in this chapter). There are a few reasons for this. First, decomposition doesn't occur readily in the type of potting mix used for Orchids. And secondly, the problem with organic fertilizers is that they can host diseases that may cause problems to your plants. So in the following section I am refering specifically to inorganic fertilizers. The most common types of orchid fertilizers are granule, slow-release, and water-soluble. There are advantages and disadvantages to each.

Granule

How to Apply: Apply as is on or in the potting matter

Advantage: Inexpensive and straightforward to use.

Disadvantage: It is a short-term fertilizer and only lasts a few weeks. Granule fertilizer can also burn roots easily. Many also lack beneficial trace elements.

Slow-Release

How to Apply: Apply as is on or in the potting matter.

Advantage: Can last anywhere from 3-9 months.

Disadvantage: More expensive than granule fertilizer. It can also burn orchid roots and may be washed out of potting matter that is too coarse.

Water-Soluble

How to Apply: Must be diluted and applied using a watering can. It is very important to dilute it according to manufacturer directions.

Advantage: Plants receive the nutrients instantly. Easy to apply.

Disadvantage: The solution must be applied every few weeks when plants are in active growth.

NEVER:

- Apply more than the recommended dose.
- Fertilize orchids that are sick/in poor condition.
- Fertilize orchids with root damage.
- Apply fertilizer to dry potting matter.

ALWAYS:

- Read and follow manufacturer instructions.
- Apply fertilizer only when the potting matter is wet.
- Fertilize orchids in active growth.
- Remove excess salts: Drench the potting matter with water every few weeks to wash out excess fertilizer minerals (this process is often called leaching).
- Remove crusted salt minerals from pots with damp cloths. (These deposits can actually burn the orchids.)

Some experienced growers prefer to fertilize their plants more often using diluted solutions rather than fertilizing the full doses less frequently. This is a more "natural" solution, but it should be done with caution—monitor the amount of fertilizer carefully.

Fertilizer Burn:

Over-fertilizing your orchid, applying fertilizer when the potting matter is dry and/or letting excess salt build up can damage your orchid's roots and leaves. The salt minerals in the fertilizer will dehydrate the roots and cause what is known as fertilizer burn.

What does fertilizer burn look like?

You will find brown or black root tips and/or leaf tips. Again, only fertilize when the potting matter is damp. You can trim root tips and/or leaf tips with a sterilized cutting tool. See Chapter 5 to learn how cinnamon and/or Listerine can help protect newly cut leaves and roots.

And now, as promised one of the best kept secrets among experienced orchid growers:

The perfectly safe, 100% all-natural "fountain of youth" and Orchid growth "steroid" combined into one!

When I came across this, I remember my eyes lit up with excitement and I could not WAIT to try it on my own plants. I had heard about other people having success, but when I tried it myself, what I experienced just blew my mind. The "secret ingredient" that I'm talking about is what's known as "worm tea." Basically, worm tea is concentrated extract of worm composted in liquid form. It's created by running water through a bed of worms in composting material, and there was some research a few years ago out of Ohio State University concluding that you could greatly accelerate plant growth in general by spraying it on food crops. Worm tea has only recently made its way into the world of growing Orchids, so this is some real "insider stuff." :)

There are a number of retailers online that offer

worm tea, or you can actually make it yourself if you have the time and patience. Simply do a Google search for "worm tea" or "worm castings" and you'll find several online retailers as well as sites explaining how to make it yourself. One shop that specializes in worm tea, and where I've purchased from before is Our Vital Earth, which can be found at http://www.ourvitalearth.com.
If you use a concentrate, you'll want to dilute it with water in a ratio of about 50 to 1.

I tried using it at first in one my phals about once every two weeks, and the results were impressive. The leaves of the plant started appearing much heartier, and greener than another phal that I'd purchased together with it. After 3 months, the "worm tea" phal had outgrown his counterpart by about 2 inches, and remained in bloom an extra 3 weeks.

Now I use worm tea on all of my plants, and the best part is that worm tea is also a natural fungicide and pesticide. So now I'm also misting the leaves and flowers of all my plants, usually about every other week. Not only is this a great way to fertilize your plants, but it will also help build up their immune system to insects and disease, which is also great segue into the next chapter...

Chapter 5

Pests & Diseases

In this chapter, we'll be covering the following topics:

• Preventing pests & diseases
• Identifying & treating common pests
• Identifying & treating common bacteria and diseases

Preventing Pests and Disease:

Prevention is the best medicine! In the previous chapter, we talked about a great all-natural way of preventing disease in your plants. Here are some other tips to keep your beautiful orchids pest and disease free:

• Purchase healthy plants that will thrive in your particular growing environment.

• Always use sterilized tools especially when you are cutting roots, leaves and/or stems. Intense heat (flame) or a diluted solution of bleach can be used to sterilize your tools.

• Grow your orchid in the environment it needs.

• Orchids are more susceptible to disease when they are under stress and living in the wrong temperature, lighting and humidity conditions.

• Always water your plants early in the day to allow for all water to dry before cooler nighttime temperatures. Use cotton swabs to remove excess water.

• Never let orchids/pots sit in water—this causes root rot.

• Do not overcrowd orchids—make sure there is adequate air circulation around them.

• Inspect your orchid regularly. Keep an eye on new growth and check your leaves (including below your leaves) for any evidence of pests.

• Always repot your orchids in new potting matter and new (or sterilized) pots.

• Always quarantine new orchids for at least 3 weeks to prevent them from spreading any diseases/insects to your older plants.

• Keep the growing area clean and remove any dead leaves and dry flowers.

IMPORTANT TIP: *When it comes to horticultural oils, do not use dormant oils. Superior oils, like brand name SunSpray Ultra-Fine are thinner and better for plants in active growth.*

Identifying & Treating Common Pests:

The following chart will help you identify and treat some of the most common orchid pests you may encounter while growing orchids. Most solutions will require multiple treatment applications. I've numbered the solutions for each problem below, and you should start with solutions listed next to #1 before working your way down to #2 (I've included the more commonly used / least harmful solutions first).

WARNING: *Chemical insecticide should only be used as last resort—and be sure to spot spray on the effected areas only if possible.*

Scale Insects

Symptoms:

These insects are typically found under leaves (near edges or the central vein) and can also be found on flower stems. Leaves may show some yellow spots on the surface.

Solutions:

Scale insects are difficult to eliminate completely but they can be controlled by repeatedly treating the insects. You must penetrate the shell of the insect or the shell must be removed in order to kill the insect. You can remove the shell by rubbing your fingers over the insect.

1. Isopropyl alcohol—apply with a cotton swab. Or try Orange Guard.
2. Insecticidal Soap. Horticultural oil. Neem.

Mealy Bugs

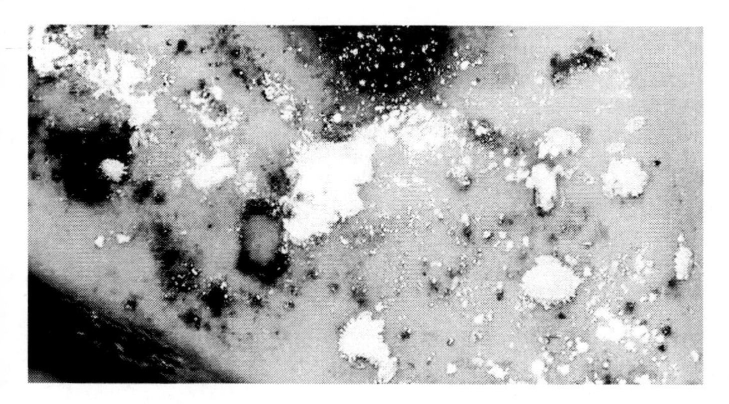

Symptoms:

Mealy bugs can be removed through persistent treatment. Easily spotted, cotton like bundles will be found on the buds, flower stems, growing tips and possibly even on the roots. A female can lay between 100-200 eggs that will hatch in 2 weeks. Inspect your plants for the eggs, look for a cottony residue.

Solutions:

1. Isopropyl alcohol—apply with a cotton swab.
2. Insecticidal soap. Horticultural oil. Neem.

(For mealy bugs on roots: Soak the roots in insecticidal soap for a few hours and then repot with new potting matter and a new pot.)

Spider Mites

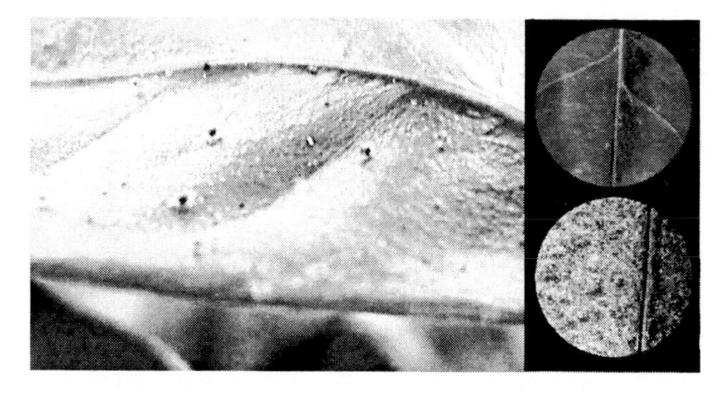

Symptoms:

Tiny, hard to see green or red spiders. You can determine if they are present by rubbing a whit cloth over the damaged area. A brown residue will be left on the leaf if mites and/or mite eggs are present. Fine webs can be seen in extreme cases. Spider mites often appear in dry and hot conditions. They feed off the sap in the leaves resulting in a stippling effect on the leaves.

Solutions:

1. Wash off with warm water.
2. Insecticidal soap. Horticultural oil. Orthene

Aphids

Symptoms:

Aphids come in all colors—green, red, black, yellow, etc—and are usually found feeding in clusters on new shoots, leaves and flower buds. Aphids can do extensive damage by deforming flower buds.

Solutions:

1. Wash off with warm water.
2. Insecticidal soap. Orange Guard. Horticultural oil. Isopropyl alcohol.

(Do not use chemicals/insecticide to remove aphids on flower buds—this must be a last resort as the chemicals may further damage flower buds/flowers.)

Thrips

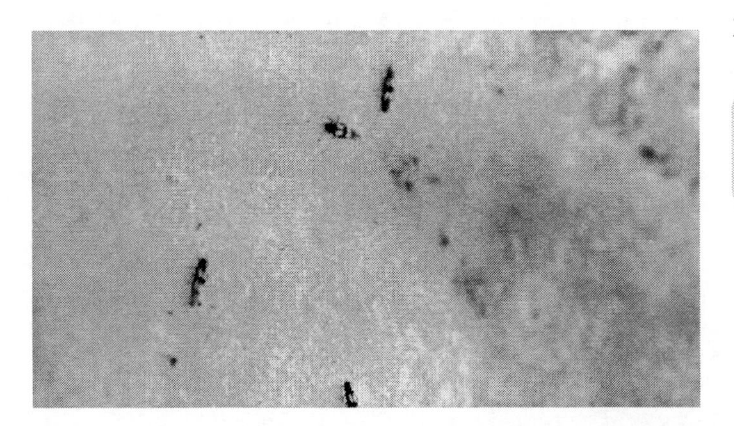

Symptoms:

Thrips are also very difficult to spot. They are elongated, gnat-like pests. Thrips come in all kinds of colors, but green and black thrips are most common on orchids. Thrips feed off of sap and target flower buds, flowers and leaves. This will lead to deformed flower buds, streaks on flowers and stippling on leaves.

Solutions:

1. Neem. Horticultural oil. Insecticidal soap.
2. Malathion. Orthene.

Slugs & Snails

Symptoms:

Snails and slugs can do major damage by eating holes in young roots, stems, flowers and leaves. They enjoy cool, damp spots and mainly come out at night. Be sure to inspect the bottom of your pots and look for any "slime trails".

Solutions:

1. Lettuce Trap: Place a piece of lettuce out to attract the snails/slugs. They will feed on the lettuce and you can then simply remove them. Beer: Fill a shallow container with about ½ inch of beer. The snails/slugs will approach the beer and drown. (Snails and slugs are attracted to the yeast.)
2. Sluggo

***IMPORTANT TIP:** Keep pollinating insects away from flowering orchids; the flowers will collapse soon after they are pollinated.*

Ants

Ants are not considered to be orchid pests because they do not damage the plants. You can get rid of ants in the mix by completely drenching your plants in water (they will crawl out or drown). An ant problem can often be a sign that you have other pests around as ants feed off the fluid that other pests (aphids, scales and mealy bugs) leave behind. They also protect and transport these other pests. You can eliminate ants with Orange Guard. Bay leaves are also a natural ant repellent and can be placed around the point of entry and in the pots to keep ants away.

Mice

Symptoms:

Nibbles on flower buds and on leaves.

Solutions:

1. Live traps.
2. Snap traps.

2 Useful Home Remedies

Cinnamon is a natural fungicide that can be applied to broken or newly cut roots. Simply wet the cut roots and apply a light dusting of regular baking cinnamon over the roots. The roots should be wet so the cinnamon sticks—you can even use a little alcohol in place of water. Too much cinnamon can inhibit root growth, do not use on regular, healthy, uncut roots.

Listerine (original gold colored) has anti-fungal properties and the alcohol content also makes it effective against bugs. It can be used as a spray (at full strength) for short periods (2-3 days is ok) as a preventative.

Fungal/Viral Problems

Fungal/Bacterial Diseases

Symptoms:

Fungal/Bacterial diseases often leave behind circulars spots or elongated streaks on leaves and flowers. Pseudobulbs may have brown or black bruises and the center growing point, or crown, may turn black and/or rot leading to death. Each symptom can usually be used to identify the type of disease.

Examples...

Fungal Rot:

Brown/Black irregular spots on leaves or pseudobulbs.

Rhizhome Rot:

Psuebobulbs have black or brown bruises.

Crown Rot:

Center and young leaves are mushy and black.

Solution:

If the problem is not too severe, the affected areas can be removed with a sterilized cutting tool, then disinfected and treated with a fungicide.
Recommended mild fungicides/bactericides are Natriphene, Physan20, Phyton 27, or RD-20.

Viral Infections

Viral infections are hard to detect. Unfortunately viral infections have no practical cures.

Examples...

Borytis fungus shows signs of flower spotting. The problem is more common during the cooler months and is more obvious on light colored flowers. Raising the temperature may keep the problem from recurring.

Mosaic Virus shows signs of color streaks on flowers.

Other virus infection symptoms include circular blackened rings on stems and leaves and elongated streaks on leaves or pseudobulbs.

Removing Infected Areas

Always use a sterilized blade. You should sterilize your blade eithe with a diluted bleach solution or under a flame (I personally prefer a flame, because it avoids potential plant reactions to the chemical.) If you use a flame, just be sure to let the blade sufficiently cool. Whenever you're handling your plants, you should also thoroughly wash your hands with anti-bacterial soap, and if you want to be extra cautious you can wear latex gloves.

You can remove the infected, diseased roots/leaves by cutting off about ½ to 1 inch into the healthy leaf/root. Do not cut into an infected area and then a healthy area—this will only spread the disease. You can then treat the cut edge with a fungicide. Some mild fungicides/bactericides include: Natriphene, Physan20, Phyton 27, or RD-20.

Other Toxic Problems

Symptoms:

Spotted leaves or pseudobulbs.

Likely cause:

Contaminant in the air—aerosols, cooking fumes, smoke.

Symptoms:

Black root tips, Brown/Black leaf tips

Likely cause:

Potting orchids in a decorative pot or container not designed for orchids. This is a toxic reaction due to the metal based glazes found on decorative pots. The roots and leaves are poisoned by the metals found in the glaze. It is best to leave orchids in clay or plastic pots and then position them in decorative pots for display purposes only. Do not repot them into a more decorative pot that can expose the roots/leaves to toxic surfaces.

More information on pests and disease can be found in Orchid Pests and Diseases by the American Orchid Society (which is available through various retailers online).

Chapter 6

Blooming & Reblooming

In this chapter, we'll be covering the following topics:

• Blooming frequency and length of blooming period for common Orchids
• Orchids with especially long blooming periods
• How to get your Orchid to bloom as long as possible, and rebloom year after year
• The top 9 reasons why an Orchid won't bloom or re-bloom
• How to cut and rebloom a phalaenopsis

Blooming Basics:

With good reason, one of the biggest areas of concern among Orchid growers is how to get your orchid to bloom longer, and bloom again and again, year after year. After all, at the end of the day, for most of us this is what it's all about – enjoying those gorgeous blooms which make all the work involved with orchid care worth it. Caring for orchids is a multi-dimensional challenge, and to get your orchid blooming for as long as possible, and repeatedly year after year, things need to be firing on all cylinders. Everything that we've covered in the book so far is crucial to making this happen – proper light, temperature, humidity, watering, fertilizer, etc. But this chapter will focus on the topic of blooming in a bit more detail.

How often are orchids supposed to bloom in a year? How long do flowers typically last? What season will my orchid be in bloom?

If you're having problems getting your orchid to bloom, before trying to diagnose whether you have a problem on your hands, you should first know the natural blooming cycle of your particular orchid. Certain varieties only bloom once a year, and their blooming period can be quite brief. Whereas other varieties can rebloom up to several times per year, and if cared for properly will be in bloom for much of the year.

The following bloom chart answers these most frequently asked questions regarding orchids and blooming:

Orchid	Number of Days in Bloom	Bloom Frequency	Normal Season
Cattleya	7-12+	1 time a year	Spring or Autumn (some Summer or Winter)
Cymbidium	30-45+	1 time a year	January to March (some July & August)
Dendrobium	30-45+	1-2 times a year	January to March
Oncidium	30-45+	1-2 times a year	January to March
Paphiopedilum	60-90+	1-2 times a year	Different times in the year
Phalaenopsis	60-120+	1-2 times a year	January to March
Vanda	30-90+	2-3 times a year	Spring through Autumn (& year round)

**Months listed refer to Northern Hemisphere*

REMEMBER: *When you purchase an orchid already in bloom, you should try to determine how long the flower has already been in bloom. If the expected blooming period is 30 days and the plant has already been in bloom for 25 days, you'll likely only enjoy blooms for a couple more days. The safest bet is to purchase a budding plant, which is about to enter into its blooming period. A good specialist orchid supplier will be more than willing to provide you with this information before you purchase your plant.*

How can I get my orchids to bloom all year long?

The only way to ensure you have orchids blooming all year long is to grow different types of orchids that bloom at different times of the year. Unfortunately, most orchids only bloom in specific seasons. *Phalaenopsis* for instance generally bloom between January to March—nothing, no matter what you do will make it bloom year round.

Some orchids do bloom longer than others, the following are just a few orchids that can bloom for long periods/in constant bloom:

• *Pleurothallis hypnicola* (not a beginner orchid, difficult to grow)
• *Epidendrum* species (easier than Pleurothallis orchids)
• *Spathoglottis plicata* (common, easy to grow orchid)

How can I get my blooms to last as long as possible?

6 Secrets to Longer Lasting Blooms

1. The flowers will need water to stay healthy—keep your plants well watered.

2. Prevent spotting or diseases—do not mist your flowers or keep your flowering plants in conditions that are too humid without the proper air circulation.

3. Keep your flowering plants out of harsh, direct sunlight.

4. Flowers enjoy cooler temperatures—not above 75ºF (24ºC)

5. Keep flying insects away—the flowers will die soon afterwards if a bee or other insect pollinates them.

6. Keep flowers away from air pollutants and ripe fruit. Flowers can fade/collapse if they are exposed to air pollutants such as smoke, paint thinner or aerosol sprays and ethylene gas that is released from ripening fruit. Orchids should be kept at least 10 feet away from ripening fruit.

My orchid won't bloom or I can't get it to rebloom. What am I doing wrong?

As I mentioned in the intro to this chapter, basic orchid care conditions must be met for orchids to bloom and rebloom. They will need the correct light, temperature and humidity conditions. The following are the most common reasons why orchids don't bloom/rebloom. The list is in order from most common to least common reason. You should use this checklist to diagnose your problem, walking through the list in order, starting with #1. Refer to the relevant sections in this book for how to address each issue.

The 9 Most Common Reasons Why You Can't Get Your Orchid To Bloom or Rebloom:

1. Temperature differential between daytime/nighttime temperatures is inadequate

2. Wrong temperature: too cold or too warm

3. Not enough light

4. Not enough water

5. Not using fertilizer (or using the wrong kind of fertilizer)

6. Overwatering in cold temperatures

7. Not enough humidity

8. Pests and/or disease

9. Young and/or recently divided orchids

How do I cut and rebloom a phalaenopsis?

One of the most impressive features about *Phalaenopsis* orchids is their ability to rebloom over and over. A new spike can grow from a finished flower spike naturally. Alternatively, a new spike can be forced to develop by cutting below the bottom flower. (However, some orchid growers have a general rule that stems should not be cut unless they are dry and dead.) Look for the node where the first flower bloomed (the bottom flower closest to the leaves, not at the tip). You will want to cut the spike with a sterilized blade back to the first node (bump in the stem) below where this first flower bloomed. A new flower spike will then emerge from this node. Cut only once the flower spike is finished blooming/flowering.

WORD OF CAUTION: *Blooming your orchid repeatedly can exhaust your orchid and may result in damaged leaves and/or flowers. You can provide your plant with rest simply by cutting off a bloomed flower spike at the last node or closer to the base. Your orchid will redirect its energy into producing new leaves and roots and the flowers can be enjoyed in an arrangement.*

Chapter 7

Potting Repotting & Staking

In this chapter, we'll be covering the following topics:

- Advantages & disadvantages of common potting materials for Orchids
- Proven potting mix recipes that you can make yourself
- What kind containers you should use
- How to mount your Orchid to new potting mix
- Repotting your Orchid
- How to know when it's time to repot
- When is the best time of year to repot
- How to repot your Orchid, step-by-step
- Staking your Orchid
- When is it time to stake your Orchid
- How to Stake your Orchid, step-by-step

Potting Basics

Potting Mix:

Orchid roots require more air space than dirt allows. Potting mix is often a combination of various potting elements that work best when combined together.

The following is a list of the most popular individual orchid potting elements.

Potting Matter	Advantage(s)	Disadvantage(s)
Charcoal	Decomposes slowly; absorbs contaminants	Holds very little water
Fir Bark	Inexpensive; Available in different sizes	Decomposes quickly; Takes time to moisten
Gravel	Inexpensive; Good drainage	Heavy; Holds no nutrients
Lava Rock	Good drainage; Does not decompose	Heavy
Perlite	Inexpensive; Retains water; Good aeration	Can hold too much water
Sphagnum Moss	Retains water; Good aeration	Can hold too much water (must pack tightly)
Styrofoam Peanuts	Inexpensive; Lightweight; Does not decompose; Good drainage	Best used as drainage at the bottom; Does not retain water; Holds no nutrients
Tree Fern Fiber	Decomposes slowly; Good drainage	Expensive; Holds little water

Potting Mix Recipes:

Ready-made orchid potting mixes are readily available or you can create your own. The key to making your own mix is to factor in your orchid's water requirements. Generally speaking, terrestrial orchids prefer continuously damp potting matter while epiphyte or lithophyte orchids prefer to dry out between waterings. Smaller roots will also grow better in finer, water-retentive matter and larger roots do better in coarser matter. Consider the characteristics of each potting element closely when you are creating your own potting mixes. The following are easy orchid potting mix recipes that work:

Fine Mix

Ideal for slipper orchids, oncidiums, miltonias, and other orchids with small roots that prefer damp potting matter conditions.

4 parts fine-grade fir bark
1 part fine charcoal
1 part horticultural perlite

Medium Mix

Ideal for cattleyas, phalaeonopsis, and mature orchids.

4 parts medium-grade fir bark
1 part medium charcoal
1 part horticultural perlite

> ***IMPORTANT:*** *Using New Potting Mix*
> *Both ready-made and self-mixed potting mixes must be soaked prior to use to ensure that they will hold the most moisture possible.*

How do I soak my new potting mix before using it with my new plants?

The soaking process is rather straightforward:

1. Place the potting mix you will be using in a bucket/container with room to spare (the mix will expand).

2. Fill the bucket/container with HOT water

3. Let the potting mix soak in the hot water overnight.

4. Drain the water by pouring the mix in a strainer and rinse the mix with warm water. The additional rinsing will help remove any dust and small particles.

Containers:

Clay & Plastic Pots

As already discussed in *Chapter 4*, plastic pots are good for orchids that prefer damp conditions while those that need to dry out between waterings will do better in clay pots. The orchid container should have adequate drainage with holes arranged at the bottom and/or sides. Do not pot orchids directly into decorative pots. See the end of *Chapter 5* to learn how this can damage, even kill your orchid.

> ***IMPORTANT TIP:*** *Clear plastic pots are great. You can monitor your orchid's roots easily without having to remove your orchid from the pot. Can't find them at your local garden store? Ask for some clear food containers at the prepared food section of your local supermarket or deli— just don't forget to add holes for drainage.*

Baskets

Orchids do not have to be restricted to pots. In fact, they do wonderfully in wooden and/or hanging baskets and can even be mounted on trees.

Wooden baskets (made of teak or another rot-resistant wood) and hanging baskets should first be lined with sheet moss before adding the potting mix.

How do I mount my orchid?

1. Place the plant on moist sphagnum moss, spread the roots evenly into the moss.

2. Position the orchid on the tree/mount so that the center points downwards. The center of the plant will collect water, ultimately leading to disease/rot, if it faces upwards.

3. Secure the moss and orchid to the tree/mount with stainless-steel wire or fishing line (do not secure it too tightly or it will cut into the roots).

Mounted orchids may require more frequent watering as they drain much faster than an orchid in a pot. Don't forget to inspect the orchid regularly for any signs of pests and/or disease.

Repotting

How will I know when it is time to repot?

There are a few telltale signs for knowing when to repot.

Sign #1:
Orchid roots are overflowing over the edges of the pot/container

Sign #2:
Potting matter no longer drains properly (the matter stays really soggy).

Sign #3
Orchid has grown over the edge of the pot.

What is the best time of year to repot?

Most orchids should be repotted in the spring months once the plant starts new growth—you'll see new roots, or shoot—and after it flowers. For example, Cattleyas are best repotted after they've flowered, the plant has reached the edge of the pot and the new roots are at least 1 inch long. Repotting an overgrown orchid can be done but will be slightly more difficult as one must be careful to avoid breaking the roots and new growth.

How do you repot an orchid?

Before you begin, make sure that you've sterilized all tools and either thoroughly washed your hands or use disposable latex gloves when handling your orchid.

Step 1:
Turn the orchid/pot, upside-down with one hand held over the potting material.

Step 2:

Tap the bottom of the pot and/or use a knife or other thin object to lightly scrape around the edges of the potting matter. Gently remove the orchid from the pot and remove old potting matter from the roots with your hands.

Step 3:

Remove old, loose, damaged/diseased roots with a sterilized cutting tool.

Step 4:

If the roots are healthy, position the orchid in a pot (one size larger than the previous pot) with the old growth towards the back so that the new growth has space to grow (frontwards). Monopodial orchids (orchids that grow upwards rather than sideways) should be repotted at the center of the container.

If many roots are damaged/diseased and have to be removed, repot the orchid in a new clean, sterilized pot of the same size (or smaller if necessary).

Step 5:

Place the plant so that the new shoots are level with the pot rim. Position it as the same depth as it was prior to repotting.

Step 6:

Fill the bottom of the pot with a layer of Styrofoam peanuts to ensure proper drainage (optional) and then add fresh potting matter. You can pack the matter around the orchid roots with your fingers. The orchid should be secure.

Step 7:
Place a wooden stake at the center of the pot and tie new and old leaves carefully with string. See the next section in this chapter for instructions on properly staking stems with flower spikes.

NOTE: *The photos in this section were taken from a video excerpt from a helpful Orchid Care DVD, by Willowbee Orchids, which you can learn more about and purchase at http://Orchids86.com.*

Staking

When is the best time to stake?

The #1 most important thing is to stake before orchids have flowered!

How do you properly stake an orchid?

Spray Orchids like *Phalaenopsis* and *Oncidiums*:

Step 1:
Start when the flower spike is about 12 inches long, insert a vertical stake as close to where the spike emerges from at the base.

Step 2:
Attach a twist-tie (not damaging wire) near the first node (bump in the stem) and then another a few inches higher.

Step 3:
Continue to add ties as the flower spike grows. The last tie should be 2-3 inches below where the first flower bud is forming.

Properly staked *Phalaenopsis*

IMPORTANT TIP: *Baby hair clips can also be used in place of twist-ties. They do not harm your plants like some wires may and add a decorative element—they are available in many colors and shapes including flowers, butterflies, birds, etc. which can be used as an attractive way of displaying your flowers.*

Orchids with single or few flowers per spike like *Cattleyas* and *Paphiopedilums*:

Step 1:

Insert a stake as close to where the spike emerges from at the base.

Step 2:

Attach a twist-tie at the base and a few inches below the first flower bud.

Chapter 8

Introduction to Propagation

In this chapter, we'll be covering the following:

- Dividing Sympodial Orchids
- Propagating Keikis
- Topping an Orchid
- Propagating from cuttings
- Propagating from backbulbs
- Propagating from seeds (warning, don't try this at home)

Propagation Basics:

If you're not familiar with the term, plant propagation simply means the production of more plants by seeds, cuttings, grafting or other methods. Orchid propagation is more of an advanced topic, and one that would require an entire book to cover it fully. That being said, we'll be covering some of the basic techniques in this chapter because eventually as your Orchids mature and you become more comfortable working with your plants, you'll probably want to begin propagating your own favorite plants.

Dividing Sympodial Orchids

(orchids that grow sideways like Cattleyas)

When should I divide my plant?

You can divide your orchid plant when it has grown too big and/or the rhizomes (creeping stems) are growing over each other and look like they are tangled.

How do I properly propagate my orchid?

Multiplying your plants is relatively easy to do. Orchids should be divided with at least 3 or 4 psuedobulbs (growths) per section/new pot. Typically, the larger the division the better. The rhizome should be cut with a sterilized sharp knife or blade. Once divided, your orchids can be repotted into smaller containers following the steps in *Chapter 7*.

Keikis

What is a Keiki anyway?

A keiki, is a baby orchid that sprouts off a flower spike or pseudo-bulb of mature orchids like *Phalaenopsis*.

When is the right time to separate and transplant a keiki?

Do not cut the keiki from the stem until the baby plant has developed a few roots at least 2 inches long. You can then cut the plant from the flower spike using a sterilized blade (leave an inch or two on each side) and then repot in a small container following the steps in *Chapter 7*. Some growers also prefer to keep the keiki on the mother plant until it falls off on its own. Make sure to mist the keiki's roots regularly to keep it hydrated if you choose to keep it growing on the mother plant.

Topping an Orchid

What do people mean when they say "topping an orchid"?

Some tall orchids may grow roots above ground from their stems. Like a keiki, you can create more plants by cutting the stem just below new roots (trying to keep as many of the new roots intact as possible). Once you've cut the stem, you'll want to repot it in fresh potting matter (follow the steps in Chapter 7). Repotting this top orchid is referred to as "topping an orchid". The original mother plant should stay in the original container—in fact, it may even continue to sprout new baby plants.

Cuttings

What exactly are cuttings?

Some orchids have cane-like long stems. These stems can be cut into pieces (or cuttings) that can be used to grow new plants.

Okay, so how do I propagate my orchid using cuttings?

The process is relatively straight-forward, but you need a little patience to wait for the cuttings to grow.

Step 1:

Remove a cane/stem from the original plant with a sterilized blade.

Step 2:

Divide the cane (again, with a sterilized blade) into sections. Each section must have at least two nodes (bumps visible by the circular line that divides the cane).

Step 3:

Lay the newly cut stems horizontally in a container filled with a bed of damp sand or sphagnum moss and cover the container with glass or plastic to trap the moisture. Then, place the container in a warm area (70-75ºF/21-24ºC) and bright light (but not direct sunlight). You can also place the cuttings 6 inches beneath a two-tube fluorescent light fixture.

New plants will sprout within a few months. The plants can then be repotted when the roots are a few inches long (see *Chapter 7*).

Back Bulbs

What's a back bulb and what kind of orchids have them?

Backbulb is the term for the older, leaf-less stems of orchids that have already flowered. Orchids like cymbidiums and oncidiums have backbulbs. The backbulb does not develop new growth when left in a pot, but it may sprout new growth if it is removed from the original plant.

How do I propogate using back bulbs?

Step 1:

Remove all backbulbs without leaves.

Step 2:

Fill a plastic bag with a 2-3 inch layer of sphagnum moss. Place as many backbulbs in the bag that fit comfortably so that the bottom ¼ of the bulbs are buried in the moss. Seal the bag.

Step 3:

Place the bag in a warm area (70-75ºF/21-24ºC) and bright light (not direct sunlight). New growth will develop in about two months.

Step 4:

Once the new leaves have grown a few inches, the bulbs can be moved into a shallow container where they will continue to grow in indirect sunlight. The bulbs can be individually repotted in several months.

Seeds

WARNING: Do NOT try this at home

Growing orchids from seeds is an extremely difficult task. The tiny orchid seeds have little food storage and therefore rely on a specific fungus for germination and development. Today, orchid seeds are germinated in laboratories where conditions can be controlled. It may take an orchid anywhere from 1 to 12 years to go from germination to flowering. Most orchids do flower around four years after germination. Growing orchids from seeds is not recommended for beginners.

Part II

Ultimate Orchid FAQs & Troubleshooting Guide

Note about this section

This FAQ & Troubleshooting section is designed as a quick and easy way to to just "get the information you're looking for." You'll find that some (but not all) of the questions are also covered within Part I of this book. You can use this FAQ & Troubleshooting guide to quickly and easily jump right to the info you're looking for, and skip over the stuff that's not important to you rat the moment. If you have a question that's not covered, please let me know at Ryan@OrchidsMadeEasy.com because we're always looking for ways to improve this guide.

Your First Orchids

1. What separates orchids from other plants?

The column. The reproductive parts—the stamen (male) and pistil (female)— are fused together to form the single column structure.

2. Do orchids have fragrant flowers?

Not all orchids have a smell. Some have delicate smells of rose, vanilla and jasmine, while others are even known to smell of decay. See *Appendix I* for some of the many wonderfully scented orchids and the bit about the "World's Worst Smelling Orchid."

3. Are orchids expensive?

Fortunately, orchids come in all price points. Beginner orchids start at about $20 (much cheaper than a flower arrangement!) while specialty award winning plants can cost hundreds to thousands of dollars. Check out the resource list included in the *Appendix* for recommended orchid retailers.

4. Are orchids difficult to grow?

This is by far one of the greatest misconceptions about orchids. Orchids are extremely sturdy plants and many can be kept in the same indoor conditions alongside your other houseplants. Check out *Chapters 3 &*

4, to read about how to properly care for your orchid.

5. Do I need a greenhouse or can I grow orchids indoors?

Orchids can be grown in greenhouses, shade houses, indoors and outdoors. Again, the key to having a healthy, happy orchid is to ensure that it is growing in the proper environment it needs. Read more about environment care conditions in *Chapter 3*.

6. My first orchid: I just bought an orchid/received one as a gift, how do I care for it?! How do I keep it alive?!

The first immediate thing you should do is make sure that your orchid has been watered. Run your plant under the faucet/or use a watering can until all of the potting material is moist. Make sure all of the water drains out—do not leave your pot sitting in water. You should water with warm/room temperature water and only in the morning to ensure any water on your plant dries by nighttime. Once you plant has been watered, you should proceed by reading *Chapters 3 &4* or *Orchid Cheat Sheets* which will walk you through step-by-step on the other care your specific orchid requires.

7. What are the best orchids for beginners?

This is a great question! Growing orchids in your home can be extremely rewarding, there is no greater feeling than watching your plant thrive! There are tons of orchids on the market and narrowing down the choices can seem daunting. The following are some of the best orchids for beginners.

Best Orchids For Beginners:

Remember, the easiest orchid to grow will be the one that will thrive the best in your particular home/outdoor environment. Learn more about how to assess your environment and properly care for orchid by reading *Chapters 3 & 4* in this book.

Phalaenopsis
Paphiopedilums

These are also good, but require more light for reblooming:

Cattleyas

Dendrobiums
Oncidiums

Check out the Orchid Cheat Sheets for specific care requirements for each variety.

8. How and where can I purchase a specific variety of orchid?

Orchids have become so incredibly popular you no longer have to stick to the varities available in your local area. Orchids can be purchased from Orchid Suppliers, Orchid Shows and even on websites such as http://www.orchidweb.org/marketplace.html and Orchid Mall http://www.orchidmall.com. See the resource list in the *Appendix* for a list of Orchid Suppliers and Orchid Shows.

9. Are there any orchids that are constantly or almost always in bloom?

Some orchids do bloom longer than others, the following are just a few orchids that can bloom for long periods/in constant bloom:

Pleurothallis hypnicola (not a beginner orchid, difficult to grow)
Epidendrum species (easier than Pleurothallis orchids)
Spathoglottis plicata (common, easy to grow orchid)

See *Chapter 6* in this book for more information about blooming.

How To Identify Your Orchid

1. How do I identify what type of orchid plant I have, so I can look up what kind of care they require?

If your orchid did not arrive with a label, trying find out where the orchid came from. You will be able to get the name with a quick phone call to the nursery or florist or a look at their website.

Most discount stores, local nurseries and florists sell primarily beginner orchids. Refer to the "Best Orchid for Beginners" section and/or *Orchid Cheat Sheets* to learn whether you have one of these popular species in your home.

If you don't own a beginner orchid or are trying to find the name of the exact hybrid or specialty orchid you have you may want to try asking an orchid specialist or other orchid growers. You can start with your local orchid society or nursery.

You can also post photos of your orchid on Orchid Forums/Boards and ask other members to help you identify your orchid. Do a google.com search for orchid forums, a few sites include: http://www.orchidforums.net/, http://www.orchidboard.com/community/, and http://www.orchidgeeks.com/ .

This internet orchid species photo encyclopedia is also helpful: http://www.orchidspecies.com

Your Environment

1. What climate can orchids grow outside in?

You may find that your orchid may thrive in your natural outdoor environment, for example, some orchids can live outdoors in Florida, Texas and California for most if not the entire year. If you live in an area that experiences freezing temperatures in winter, you may have no option but move your plants indoors until the harsh weather passes. Fortunately, you can enjoy your plants outdoors in the summer when the temperature rises and the humidity levels increase. The summer sun can be particularly harsh, you can protect your orchid from the sun's rays by placing them in a naturally shady location.

2. What type of orchid can I grow outdoors in my climate?

Balancing your orchid's temperature, lighting, humidity and air movement needs is key to their outdoor survival. See *Chapter 3* to determine what type of orchid can spend the year/or part of the year outdoors.

3. What type of orchid can I grow in my home?

Most orchids thrive in temperature conditions human finds comfortable—making them ideal houseplants.

Your orchid will only thrive within its temperature requirements. See Chapter X to learn more about the environment your orchid needs.

4. Can I grow different types of orchids together on the same windowsill or in the same orchid house?

Different kinds of orchids may require different environments. Therefore, the same windowsill or orchid house may not be ideal for all of your orchids. It is important that you take each orchid's specific care requirements into account. See *Chapters 3 & 4* for more information on Orchid Care or check out our *Orchid Cheat Sheets.*

5. How do I keep my orchid alive and healthy in all seasons (and for future seasons)?

Orchids require different care throughout the year—watering, light, fertilizing and repotting are just a few of the care aspects that might need changing. Check out the yearly care guide and/or Orchid Care/Cheat Sheets for more information.

Temperature

1. What temperatures do orchids prefer?

Orchids are usually classified into three different temperature categories:

Cool: 45°F to 55°F (7.2°C to 12.8°C)
Intermediate: 55°F to 60°F (12.8°C to 15.6°C)
Warm: 65°F (18.3°C) or higher

See the chart in *Chapter 3* to find the ideal temperature conditions for your specific orchid.

2. How do I grow warm-growing orchids in a cold environment?

Unfortunately, a warm-growing orchid cannot be tricked into growing in a cold environment. You must make adjustments and use heaters to keep the temperatures within their growing range. Follow all of the other orchid care requirements—especially humidity and light.

3. What happens if the temperature is too warm?

Orchids can survive short periods of extreme heat if the humidity is high enough. Prolonged periods of extreme heat will result in the slowing, even stopping of growth, wilting flowers and buds and shriveled leaves and stems.

4.What happens if the temperature is too cold?

Orchids in cooler than recommended conditions may be more susceptible to disease, have slower growth, and may suffer from bud blast—when buds fall off the stem before they have the chance to open.

Light

1. How much sunlight do they need?

Most orchids are happy in indirect light. Do not place an orchid directly in the sun—the temperature and humidity levels (especially in the summer) are not ideal for orchids. A bright window can be shaded with a sheer curtain. The chart in *Chapter 3* will help you identify the necessary light requirements.

2. Can orchids be grown under lights? How much artificial light do they need?

Yes! Orchids can be grown under artificial lights that meet their regular light requirements (and other care conditions). The chart in *Chapter 3* will help you identify the necessary light requirements.

3. Which lights work best?

See the section in *Chapter 3* for examples of the types of artificial lights that work best for orchids in each light category.

Humidity

1. How much humidity do my orchids need?

Most orchids thrive in high humidity conditions—think 50% relative humidity or higher. See the Orchid Care/Cheat Sheets for more information.

2. Will my bathroom be too humid for my orchids?

Most homes have a relative humidity between 10-20% and most orchids require relative humidity condition of higher than 50%. It would be too general to say that all orchids can thrive in bathroom environments. It is important you provide all of the care conditions your orchid requires. Think about the temperature, light and air circulation of your bathroom in addition to the humidity level.

3. How do I increase the humidity indoors?

You have several options for raising humidity levels indoors:

1. Use a humidifier, evaporative-pad humidifiers and/or mist humidifiers will work. (Many experienced growers prefer evaporative-pad humidifers over mist humidifiers because mist humidifiers can leave mineral deposits on your plants.)

2. Mist your plants, do not soak, several times a day. Like mist humidifiers, the water may leave mineral deposits on your plants. You can wipe your leaves gently if you notice any deposits.

3. Grow your plants on a humidity tray—fill tray with water and place your orchid on the grate above the tray. The humidity tray will elevate your plants above the water and it is easy to clean. You can also make your own humidity tray using pebbles. Fill a shallow tray with water and pebbles and then place your pot on the pebbles. You do not want the potting material and/or pot to soak in the water. Do keep the tray/pebbles

clean to ensure mold and/or insects do not harm your plants.

Water

1. How much water do they need? How often should I water them?

"How much water does my orchid need?" and "How often should I water them" are two of the most frequently asked questions from new, even experienced, orchid owners. Unfortunately, there is no easy answer to these questions. Many external factors must be taken into account to determine the right amount of water your specific orchid needs. Chapter 4 will show you exactly what you need to know to water your plant properly.

2. How do you water them?

Always use warm water and a water diffuser (to soften the flow if you are using a hose) or a sprinkling can. You will need to water your orchid thoroughly so that water and excess fertilizer pours out from the bottom of the pot. Do make sure your pot can continue to drain excess water if needed. NEVER let your orchid pot sit in water. This can lead to root rot and unwanted bacteria and fungus—all problems that can kill your plants.

One of the fastest ways to judge whether your plant needs more water or not is to get a rough understanding of how heavy your plant is when it is saturated with water. You can pick up your orchid again in a day or two and see just how heavy it remains. Your plant will get lighter as more of the water either absorbs or evaporates. Keep a mental note of your orchid's weight so that next time you'll know simply by picking it up that it needs more water.

You can also determine whether your plant is damp or dry by sticking your finger or a bamboo skewer into 1-2 inches of the potting matter. If you have a Phalaeonopsis (or other orchid that needs damp potting matter) and find that the potting matter is dry, you'll know that it is time to water. The bamboo skewer will come out cool or moist if the potting matter is still damp.

3. Should I mist or water? Or both?

You should not mist flowers when they are bloom. You can mist leaves and keiki's—especially in warm, dry conditions. Misting regularly can also be done when you need to raise the humidity levels around your plant.

4. How can you tell if you are giving them the right amount of water?

Both overwatering and underwatering can cause damage, even lead to killing an orchid. Your orchids will definitely show signs of water damage. For instance, pleated, pluckered, soft, yellow and droopy leaves are all signs of underwatering. Other orchids may suffer from shriveling psuedobulbs and bud blast (buds fall off). Unfortunately, these symptoms can also appear if the orchids are overwatered or exposed to hot temperatures for long periods.

5. How can I tell if I am overwatering or underwatering?

The best way to determine whether your orchid is sick due to overwatering or underwatering is to remove the plant from the pot and look directly at the roots. This is a must if you want to keep your orchid healthy. Soggy, dark, mushy, rotting, foul smelling roots are a clear sign of overwatering. Dry and shriveled roots will be seen if your plant has not gotten enough water. Turn to *Chapter 4* to learn how to inspect your orchid's roots.

6. My orchid has been overwatered. It has soggy, dark and mushy roots. What can I do?

Turn to *Chapter 4* for more information.

7. My orchid has been underwatered. It has dry, shriveled roots. What can I do?

Turn to *Chapter 4* for more information.

8. How can I remove hard water spots on my orchid's leaves?

Forget about harsh commercial products. Pineapple juice and milk can be used to rise off residue—use it straight and do a second rinse or wipe with water. Another wonderful home remedy is mayonnaise—dilute it with water and wipe it over the leaves to remove deposits and add shine to your leaves. Wipe away any excess with a water rag if necessary.

9. Can I use rainwater or dehumidifier water?

Rainwater and melted snow is great for orchids assuming you live an area that does not receive acid rain. Water collected from dehumidifiers can also be used without problems.

Potting/Mounting

1. Do orchids require a special potting matter? Can I use regular soil?

Orchid roots require more air space than dirt allows. Orchid potting mix is often a combination of various potting elements that work best when combined together. See *Chapter 7* for a list of the most popular orchid potting elements.

2. What type of growing medium is best for my orchid?

The potting matter you use for your orchids will retain water differently. For example, moss stays wetter much longer than bark does. An orchid with moss potting matter would require water less often than an orchid potted in bark. Look closely at how often your orchid needs to be watered and whether the potting matter should be damp or dry between waterings in *Chapter 4*. You can read more about potting materials in *Chapter 7*.

3. How do I make my own potting mix?

Several simple potting mix recipes are provided in *Chapter 7*.

4. What type of pot should I use? Do the pots need holes?

The type of pot your orchid is growing in plays a large part in your plant's watering schedule. Water evaporates from clay pots much faster than it does from plastic pots. This means that plants in clay pots will be watered more often than those in plastic pots.

Simply put, plastic pots are good for orchids that prefer damp conditions while those that need to dry out between waterings will do better in clay pots.

Orchid pots must have adequate holes for drainage along the bottom and/or sides. Clear plastic pots are great for keeping an eye on the condition of your roots.

5. Where can I get a clear pot?

Clear plastic pots are great. You can monitor your orchid's roots easily without having to remove your orchid from the pot. Can't find them at your local garden store? Wanna save some cash? Ask for some clear food containers at the prepared food section of your deli— just don't forget to add holes for drainage.

6. Can I pot my orchid in a decorative pot?

Never pot an orchid directly into a decorative pot. Always first place your plant in either a plastic or clay pot, and then place that pot within the decorative pot. See Chapter 5 to learn how decorative pots can be toxic to your plant.

7. How do I know when it is time to repot my orchid?

There are a few telltale signs for knowing when to repot.

a. Orchid roots are overflowing over the edges of the pot/container
b. Potting matter no longer drains properly (the matter stays really soggy).
c. Orchid has grown over the edge of the pot.

8. When is the best time of year to repot?

Most orchids should be repotted in the spring months once the plant starts new growth—you'll see new roots, or shoot—and after it flowers. For example, Cattleyas are best repotted after they've flowered, the plant has reached the edge of the pot and the new roots are at least 1 inch long. Repotting an overgrown orchid can be done but will be slightly more difficult as one must be careful to avoid breaking the roots and new growth.

9.How do I pot/repot my orchid?

A step-by-step guide to repotting can be found in *Chapter 7*.

10. What size pot should I repot my orchids in?

If many roots are damaged/diseased and need to be cut, the orchid should be repotted in a new/sterilized pot of the same size or smaller. Healthy orchids should be repotted in larger pots that will hold the plant for at least 2 years. Orchids like to be confined to small pots with not a lot of moving space—pots that are too large may keep your plant from thriving.

11. I was repotting my orchid and noticed its roots are mushy. What caused this and what should I do?

Soggy, dark, mushy, rotting, foul smelling roots are a clear sign of overwatering. See *Chapter 4* to learn how to care for severely overwatered roots.

12. My orchid's roots are dry and look dead. What caused this and what should I do?

Dry and shriveled roots will be seen if your plant has not gotten enough water. Look at the potting matter to determine if this is the cause of the problem—coarse potting materials may interact poorly with roots and lead to dehydration. If the potting matter is fine, you simply need to increase your watering frequency. See *Chapter 4* to learn how to care for severely underwatered roots.

13. My orchid's stem has leaves and roots growing from the top. Can I cut and repot the new growth?

Some tall orchids may grow roots from their stems. Like a keiki, you can create more plants by cutting the stem with new roots (try to keep as many of the new roots intact as possible) and repotting it in fresh potting matter (follow the steps in *Chapter 7*). Repotting this top orchid is referred to as "topping an orchid". The original mother plant should stay in the original container—it may even continue to sprout new baby plants.

14. I'd like to grow my orchid on a tree. How do I attach my orchid to the tree?

Not all orchids can be grown outdoors and/or on trees. Check to see whether your orchid is an epiphyte that can grow on a tree in your outdoor environment. Check to see that your orchid's care conditions will be met. Simple mounting directions are provided in *Chapter 7*.

15. Can I transplant my orchid to a wooden planter or hanging basket? If so, how do I do it?

Many epiphyte orchids can be transplanted to baskets and will do remarkably well as long as their care conditions are met. Wooden baskets (made of teak or another rot-resistant wood) and hanging baskets should first be lined with sheet moss before adding the potting mix.

Fertilizer

1. What kind of fertilizer do orchids need?

Orchids require orchid fertilizer—not regular houseplant fertilizer, not rose fertilizer, only fertilizer made for orchids. See *Chapter 4* to learn more about what you should look for in an fertilizer.

2. When and how often should I fertilize my orchid?

Over fertilizing orchids or doing so incorrectly can damage, even kill your orchid. Always read and follow manufacturer instructions. Only fertilize healthy orchids that are in active growth and only apply fertilizer when the potting matter is wet. Some growers prefer to fertilize their plants more often using diluted solutions—this is a more natural solution but should be done carefully. See Chapter 4 for more information regarding orchid fertilizers.

Blooming/Reblooming

1. Why won't my orchid bloom?

Orchids will not bloom if they are young plants, if they are outside of their regular bloom season or if they have been exposed to the wrong living conditions. Living in the environment conditions will weaken your plant and make it more susceptible to disease. See *Chapters 3 & 4* to learn how to properly care for your orchid. See *Chapter 6* to learn the 9 most common reasons your orchids won't bloom.

2. How often are orchids supposed to flower/bloom in a year?

All orchids are different—some bloom 1 time a year while other mature plants can bloom 2 to 3, even 4 times a year. See the blooming chart in *Chapter 6*.

3. How can I get my orchids to bloom as long as possible? or How do I get my orchids to bloom all year long?

It is important you provide your orchid with the proper care while it is in bloom. You can't keep your orchid in bloom year long, but you can help keep the flowers healthy. The following are tips to help your flowers last as long as possible:

1. Prevent spotting or diseases—do not mist your flowers or keep your flowering plants in conditions that are too humid without the proper air circulation.
2. Keep your flowering plants out of harsh, direct sunlight.
3. Flowers enjoy cooler temperatures—not above 75ºF (24ºC)
4. Keep flying insects away—the flowers will die soon afterwards if a bee or other insect pollinates them.
5. Keep flowers away from air pollutants and ripe fruit. Flowers can fade/collapse if they are exposed to air pollutants such as smoke, paint thinner or aerosol sprays and ethylene gas that is released from ripening fruit.

4. After the flowers fall off, what do I do with the stem? How and where should I cut it?

You can remove the stem off of most orchids once the flowers have died and fallen off. Before you cut, check the tip of the stem to see if it is dry. A dry stem is a sign that it is dying and can be cut near the base. Do not cut the stem if there are any psuedobulbs on the orchid—they are storing water and nutrients your orchid needs.

5. How do I cut and rebloom a phalaenopsis?

One of the most impressive features about phalaenopsis orchids is their ability to rebloom over and over. A new spike can grow from a finished flower spike naturally (some orchid growers have a general rule that stems should not be cut unless they are dry and dead.) A new spike can be forced to develop by cutting below the bottom flower. Look for the node where the first flower bloomed (the bottom flower closest to the leaves, not at the tip). You will want to cut the spike with a sterilized blade back to the first node (bump in the stem) below where this first flower bloomed. A new flower spike will then emerge from this node. Cut only once the flower spike is finished blooming/flowering.

Warning: Blooming your orchid repeatedly can exhaust your orchid and may result in damaged leaves and/or flowers. You can provide your plant with rest simply by cutting off a bloomed flower spike at the last node or closer to the base. Your orchid will redirect its energy into producing new leaves and roots and the flowers can be enjoyed in an arrangement.

6. How do I get my orchid to flower/bloom again, year after year?

Basic orchid care conditions must be met for orchids to bloom and rebloom. They will need the correct light, temperature and humidity conditions. See *Chapter 6* for a list of the most common reasons why orchids don't bloom/rebloom.

7. How long does it take for orchids to rebloom?

There is no exact time—it depends on the condition of the plant and the type of environment the plant is in. Some orchids may bloom only once a year while others can continue to bloom 2 to 3 times a year. See the bloom chart in *Chapter 6*. Depending on the type of orchid you have, it can take 1 to 6 months for a new flower stem to bloom once it begins to grow.

8. Some of my plants have a lot of leaves but no flowers. What should I do?

It may be that it is simply time for your plant to lose its flowers. Check to see when it should be in bloom according to the bloom chart in *Chapter 6* and care for it in the proper environment conditions. If you've just purchased your orchid and it was already in bloom, remember that you don't necessarily know how long the plant was in bloom at the orchid supplier's before taking it home with you. Also, an orchid won't flower properly if it is being stressed being exposed to the wrong temperatures or light. See *Chapter 6* for a list of the most common reason why orchids don't bloom.

Cutting/Propagation

1.When is the best time to cut the stem?

You can remove the stem off of most orchids once the flowers have died and fallen off. Before you cut, check the tip of the stem to see if it is dry. A dry stem is a sign that it is dying and can be cut near the base. Do not cut the stem if there are any psuedobulbs on the orchid—they are storing water and nutrients your orchid needs.

2. Where exactly do I cut it? How do I cut it?

A dry stem can be cut near the base. For phalaenopsis: A new spike can grow from a finished flower spike merely by cutting below the bottom flower. Look for the node where the first flower bloomed (the bottom flower closest to the leaves, not at the tip). You will want to cut the spike with a sterile blade back to the first node (bump in the stem) below where this first flower bloomed. A new flower spike will then emerge from this node. Cut only once the flower spike is finished blooming/flowering.

3. Do the roots need to be cut? How should I cut them?

Healthy roots should not be cut. Only cut damaged/diseased roots. See *Chapter 4* to learn how to do this.

4. Can I trim/cut the leaves? How?

Do not cut healthy leaves. Damaged/diseased leaves can be cut to protect the rest of the plant. See *Chapter 5* to learn how to do this.

5. What should I do when new shoots appear?

Inspect new shoots for pests regularly. Continue to care for them, but take notice if the new shoots begin to overlap or grow over the pot—it may be necessary to repot. See *Chapter 7* for more information

6. Can my orchid be divided to make new plants?

Yes! See *Chapter 8* for more information.

7. How do I divide my orchid into multiple plants?

Dividing sympodial orchids is relatively easy to do. Orchids should be divided with at least 3 or 4 psuedobulbs (growths) per section/new pot. Typically, the larger the division the better. The rhizome should be cut with a sterilized sharp knife or blade. Once divided, your orchids can be repotted into smaller containers following the steps in *Chapter 7*.

8. What is a keiki?

A keiki, is a baby orchid that sprouts off a flower spike or pseudo-bulb of mature orchids like phalaenopsis.

9. When is the right time to separate and transplant a keiki?

Do not cut the keiki from the stem until the baby plant has developed a few roots at least 2 inches long. You can then cut the plant from the flower spike using a sterile blade (leave an inch or two on each side) and then repot in a small container following the steps in *Chapter 7*. Some growers also prefer to keep the keiki on the mother plant until it falls off on its own. Do mist the keiki's roots regularly to keep it hydrated if you choose to keep it growing on the mother plant.

10. How do I take cuttings and grow new orchids?

The process is straight forward, you just need a little patience to wait for the cuttings to grow. (This information is also provided in *Chapter 8*.)

Step 1:

Remove a cane/stem from the original plant with a sterile blade.

Step 2:

Divide the cane (again, with a sterile blade) into sections. Each section must have at least two nodes (bumps visible by the circular line that divides the cane).

Step 3:

Lay the newly cut stems horizontally in a container filled with a bed of damp sand or sphagnum moss and cover the container with glass or plastic to trap the moisture. Then, place the container in a warm area (70-75ºF/21-24ºC) and bright light (not direct sunlight). You can also place the cuttings 6 inches beneath a two-tube fluorescent light fixture.

New plants will sprout within a few months. The plants can then be repotted when the roots are a few inches long (see *Chapter 7*).

11. My orchid's stem has leaves and roots growing from the top. What should I do?

Some tall orchids may grow roots from their stems. Like a keiki, you can create more plants by cutting the stem with new roots (try to keep as many of the new roots intact as possible) and repotting it in fresh potting matter (follow the steps in *Chapter 7*). Repotting this top orchid is referred to as "topping an orchid". The original mother plant should stay in the original container—it may even continue to sprout new baby plants.

12. Can I grow orchids from seeds?

Growing orchids from seeds is an extremely difficult task. The tiny orchid seeds have little food storage and therefore rely on a specific fungus for germination and development. Today, orchid seeds are germinated in laboratories where conditions can be controlled. It may take an orchid anywhere from 1 to 12 years to go from germination to flowering. Most orchids do flower around four years after germination. Growing orchids from seeds is not recommended for beginners.

Pests, Disease and Damage

1. How do I distinguish between all of the different orchid pests and diseases and figure out the right way to treat them?

Check out *Chapter 5*. You'll find a chart that will help you identify and treat the most common orchid pests.

2. What types of insects attack orchids? How can I identify the kinds on my orchid and get rid of them?

Check out *Chapter 5*. You'll find a chart that will help you identify and treat the most common orchid pests.

3.How do I kill aphids?

First Solution: Wash off with warm water. Second/Chemical Solution: Insecticidal soap. Orange Guard. Horticultural oil. Or Isopropyl alcohol.

(Do not use chemicals/insecticide to remove aphids on flower buds—this must be a last resort as the chemicals may further damage flower buds/flowers.

See *Chapter 5* for more information about other pests and diseases.

4. I have an ant problem! How do I get rid of them!?

Ants are not considered to be orchid pests because they do not damage the plants. You can get rid of ants in the mix by completely drenching your plants in water (they will crawl out or drown). An ant problem can often be a sign that you have other pests around as ants feed off the fluid that other pests (aphids, scales and mealy bugs) leave behind. They also protect and transport these other pests. You can eliminate ants with

Orange Guard. Bay leaves are also a natural ant repellant and can be placed around the point of entry and in the pots to keep ants away.

See *Chapter 5* for more information about other pests and diseases.

5. Something is eating the leaves—leaving little bite marks. What can it be? How do I stop this?!

Slugs/snails and mice can nibble leaves. See *Chapter 5* to learn how to stop these pests.

6. My orchid's roots are black and covered in mold. Why and what should I do?

Soggy, dark, mushy, rotting, foul smelling roots are a clear sign of overwatering. See *Chapters 4 & 5* to learn how to remove and treat them.

7. I've removed the mold and repotted my orchid but the mold keeps coming back. How do I get rid of it?

You will need to treat the roots with a fungicide. See *Chapter 5* for more information.

8. My orchid's roots look dry and dead. What caused this and what should I do?

Dry and shriveled roots will be seen if your plant has not gotten enough water. Look at the potting matter to determine if this is the cause of the problem—coarse potting materials may interact poorly with roots and lead to dehydration. If the potting matter is fine, you simply need to increase your watering frequency. See *Chapter 4* to learn what to do with severely underwatered orchid roots.

9. My leaves are diseased/damaged. Should I cut them? How?

You can remove diseased/damaged leaves by cutting off about ½ to 1 inch into the healthy leaf. Always use a sterilized blade and do not cut into an infected area and then a healthy area—this will only spread the disease. You can then treat the cut edge with a fungicide if necessary. Some mild fungicides/ bactericides include: Natriphene, Physan20, Phyton 27, or RD-20. See *Chapter 5* to learn how cinnamon and Listerine can help protect newly cut leaves.

Troubleshooting

1. My leaves are yellow. Why? What should I do?

The oldest leaves on a plant will yellow and drop off. Younger leaves may become yellow if they are not exposed to enough light, or are lacking a fertilizer (or one without sufficient nitrogen). See *Chapters 3 & 4* or the *Orchid Cheat Sheets* to learn more about what conditions your orchid needs.

2. My leaves are sticky. What does this mean? What can I do?

Orchid spikes often secrete a sticky substance (known as "Honeydew") and this is normal—you may also find "Honeydew" on the underside of leaves. "Honeydew" can be removed with water—simply mist/wipe and it will dissolve. Sticky substances on leaves can also be a sign of pests so it is very important to inspect them carefully for any signs. See *Chapter 5* to learn more about common orchid pests.

3. My orchid has brown/black spots on the leaves. What does this mean? What do I do?

Brown/black spots on leaves can be caused by a number of things.

Sunburn: Intense light exposure may overheat the leaves and result in sunburn. Sunburn spots are brown and round or oval in shape. A few sunburn spots on the leaves will not do any major damage, but plants can be killed if the damage covers a large area or if the center of the plant is surnburned. The sunburn mark will remain on the leaves, prevent sunburn by protecting plants from harsh sunlight.

Fungal/Bacterial diseases like fungal rot can also cause brown/black irregular spots on leaves. If the problem is not too severe, the affected areas can be removed with a sterilized cutting tool, then disinfected and treated with a fungicide. Recommended mild fungicides/bactericides are Natriphene, Physan20, Phyton 27, or RD-20. See *Chapter 5* for more information.

Black tips on leaves can be caused by overwatering or cold nighttime temperatures. Remove diseased portions and treat with anti-fungal.

Over fertilizing can also dehydrate the plant and cause black root tips and/or brown/black leaf tips.

4. My flower buds shrivel and fall off my orchids before they open. Why? What can I do?

Healthy plants that have buds fall off the stem before they have a chance to open are suffering from "bud blast". This can be caused due to rapid changes in environment (primarily wrong temperatures) and even air pollutants such as smoke, paint thinner or aerosol sprays and ethylene gas that is released from ripening fruit.

5. My flowers are withering and look wrinkled. What can I do?

Flowers wither and wrinkle before they fall off. Bulbs may be wrinkled if the plant conditions are too dry from insufficient watering or low humidity. Flowers can also be damaged due to rapid changes in environment (primarily wrong temperatures) and even air pollutants such as smoke, paint thinner or aerosol sprays and ethylene gas that is released from ripening fruit. See *Chapter 6* to learn how to best care for your flowers while they are in bloom. *Chapters 3 & 4* will provide you with the information you need to know to properly care for your orchid. Don't forget to check out the *Orchid Cheat Sheets*.

6. Why are my leaves wrinkled? How do I cure and prevent this?

Wrinkled leaves (also called accordion pleating) is a sign that the plant is not getting enough water. The humidity level may be too low, the plant may not be watered frequently enough, or the roots may be damaged and not carrying enough water. Make adjustments/treat damaged roots immediately. The leaves will be permanently damaged. (Wrinkled leaves could also be signs of other problems like overwatering—see *Chapter 4* to learn how you can tell if your plant has been overwatered.)

7. My leaves have gone floppy. What should I do?

Soft floppy leaves can be a sign of root rot caused by overwatering. See *Chapter 4* for more information about how to inspect your orchid for damaged roots and treat them.

8. I've only had my orchid a few days and all the flowers fell off! What did I do wrong?!

Healthy plants that have buds fall off the stem before they have a chance to open are suffering from bud blast. This can be caused due to rapid changes in environment (primarily wrong temperatures) and even air pollutants such as smoke, paint thinner or aerosol sprays and ethylene gas that is released from ripening fruit. The flowers may have fallen off due to similar reasons—wrong temperature, light, watering requirements. See *Chapters 3 & 4* to learn more about the proper conditions your orchid needs. It's also possible that your plant was ending its blooming cycle when you purchased it (for example, the orchid could have been in bloom for many days where you purchased the orchid). For this reason, it's best to purchase orchids with buds that are about to enter their blooming cycle. You may not be able to get this information from a supermarket or local home & garden store, but quality specialty orchid suppliers will be able and willing to provide this information for you before you purchase.

9. What is the best way to clean my orchid's leaves?

Forget about harsh commercial products. Pineapple juice and milk can be used to rise off residue—use it straight and do a second rinse or wipe with water. Another wonderful home remedy is mayonnaise—dilute it with water and wipe it over the leaves to remove deposits and add shine to your leaves. This is also a great natural way to create vibrant shiny leaves on your plant. Wipe away any excess with a water rag if necessary.

10. How can I tell if my orchid is dead or in rest?

Orchids can take months to bloom and may go dormant during some seasons. A plant is dead or dying if it has a soft, mushy or black crown (core). Bringing this orchid back to life will probably not be possible. If the leaves and roots are otherwise healthy, then it is likely that your orchid is still alive. In order for it to grow and rebloom however, you will have to ensure that you're maintaining the proper care environment for your orchid.

11.What can I immediately do if my orchid is dying?

The best thing to do is to repot it into a tight pot and provide plenty of humidity—water it and care for it as required. (Remove any diseased parts with a sterilized tool and treat before repotting.) Proper care and a bit of patience may help bring your plant back to life. See *Chapter 7* for more information about repotting.

It is very important you care for your orchid properly and provide it with the light, temperature, water, humidity and fertilizer it needs. You could be doing something that is doing more damage than good.

7 Most Common Causes of Orchid Death:

1. Overwatering
2. Underwatering
3. Leaving foliage wet overnight
4. Wrong environment
    a. wrong light intensity
    b. wrong temperature
    c. not enough humidity
d. poor air circulation
5. Pests and/or disease
6. Too much fertilizer
7. Purchase sick/already dying plants

9 Reasons Why Orchids Don't Bloom:

1. Temperature differential between daytime/nighttime temperatures is inadequate
2. Wrong temperature: too cold or too warm
3. Not enough light
4. Not enough water
5. Not using fertilizer (or using the wrong kind of fertilizer)
6. Overwatering in cold temperatures
7. Not enough humidity
8. Pests and/or disease
9. Young and/or recently divided orchids

Appendix

Ultimate Orchid Resource List

APPENDIX I:

I. FRAGRANT ORCHIDS:

Orchid:	Smells Like:
Rhynchostylis gigantea	Citrus
Cattleya walkeriana (+ hybrids)	Vanilla & Cinnamon
Angranthes grandiflora (+ hybrids)	Jasmine
Brassavola nodosa "Lady of the Night"	Freesia
Maxillaria tenuifolia	Coconut
Oncidium Sharry Baby	Chocolate
Miltoniopsis santanaei	Roses
Cymbidium Golden Elf	Lemon

World's Worst Smelling Orchid

Bulbophyllum phalaenopsis: A large orchid native to New Guinea that smells of carrion (decaying meat) and attracts flies with its unpleasant odor.

APPENDIX II:

II. ORCHID RESOURCES:

If you're looking for a one-stop resource for all things orchid, I'd recommend you first visit the following site:

http://www.orchidmall.com/index.htm

The folks at Orchid Mall have already provided an exhaustive listing of orchid resources on the internet, so I'm not going to try to replicate that here. However, one of the limitations of Orchid Mall is that it can be OVERWHELMING. When you're searching through it, you can waste literally days digging through it to find a few truly useful sites.

So in this resource list here's what I've done for you: I've provided you with both links to the exhaustive Orchid Mall site, as well as links to my own personal picks, so you can save time digging through the thousands of websites out there.

Orchid Plants:

There is a useful site that you should check out before ordering from any orchid vendor online. The site is called "Dave's Garden" but don't let the name mislead you. The site aggregates user submitted reviews of garden site vendors they've actualy dealt with, and there's a special page dedicated to orchid vendors. Just take the reviews with a grain of salt, because I've found that overall, people are more likely to post when they've had a negative experience, so you'll find a disproportionate number of negative reviews for any given vendor. But it's still useful, nevertheless. You can jump right to the orchid section at the following URL:

http://davesgarden.com/products/gwd/advanced.php?category=18&submit=Go

Orchid Supplies:

Specializes in orchid growing supplies. Great for pots, potting mixes, humidity trays, fertilizer, etc. They can be a bit pricey, but the customer service is excellent.

http://www.repotme.com/

Specializes in plant "furniture", watering trays, and plant lightboxes - bascially everything you need to display your orchids indoors.

http://www.aquastakes.com/

Orchid Forums:

My favorites, in order are:

Orchid Geeks
http://www.orchidgeeks.com/forum/

The Orchid Source
http://forum.theorchidsource.com/cgi-bin/ultimatebb.cgi

Orchid Board
http://www.orchidboard.com/

Slipper Talk (THE place for Paphiopedilum - aka "slipper" orchids) http://www.slippertalk.com/forum/index.php

GardenWeb Orchid Forum
http://forums2.gardenweb.com/forums/orchids/

Orchid Forums
http://www.orchidforums.net/

Orchid Societies

This is a useful list of Orchid Societies organized alphabetically. The list also includes geographic location of the society, which is helpful when trying to find one near you:

http://www.orchidmall.com/society.htm

Orchid identification tools:

Free Tools

Orchid Works
http://www.orchidworks.com/

Orchid Species Encyclopedia
http://www.orchidspecies.com

Paid Tools

OrchidWiz Database- ($259.00)
http://www.orchidwiz.com/servlet/StoreFront

WildCattDatabase - ($159.95)
http://www.wildcattdata.com/NewWeb/

Orchid Species Culture Sheets:

If you're looking for ultra-specific care info for your particular hybrid or specialty species, then these culture sheets may come in handy. They'll run you about $1 a piece. You can check out free sample sheets on their site.

http://www.orchidculture.com/COD/index.html